Ⓐ for Achievement
Ⓐ for Attitude
Ⓐ for Attendance

THE LIFE-CHANGING ENDEAVOUR OF NEWLANDS JUNIOR COLLEGE – A GLASGOW SUCCESS STORY

KENNY KEMP

Mereworth
publishing

Mereworth Publishing, Scotland

First published 2021 by Mereworth Publishing
Printed by Allander Print
Designed and typeset by Intrinsic.cc

British Library Cataloguing in Publication Data
A CIP catalogue record for this book is available from the British Library
ISBN: 978-1-9161762-1-8

*"There was one example of a boy in the final year.
His attendance at a previous secondary school was zero.
Yet his attendance at Newlands Junior College was 100%,"*

Scott Black, former president of Edinburgh Chamber of Commerce.

*"The issue here is about innovation in Scottish education.
No objective observer now disputes the need for significant change. Yet here
is an innovation lauded across the political spectrum that seems likely to die
because of a lack of will to see it continued,"*

Keir Bloomer, former council chief executive and educational consultant.

*"People said Newlands Junior College was like a family. It was a family. There
were no barriers and I think it is a tragic shame that it is not there now for young
people because it has transformed lives,"*

Linda McArthur, mother of former junior college student, Ross McArthur.

*"My vision was to create a Junior College for young teenagers that would give
them support and opportunity to move onto a successful and rewarding future,"*

- Jim McColl.

Contents

INTRODUCTION:
The Life-Changing Endeavour

This is a marvellously inspirational story about Newlands Junior College, a small educational establishment set up on the south side of Glasgow. For five years the college gave a group of young people who had fallen out of secondary schooling a fresh start and a new direction in learning which steered the overwhelming majority of them on to positive paths in life.

This is also a salutary tale of life in contemporary Scotland. It is the story of the conception of the junior college — as a pilot project — and the efforts to build and sustain it and the disappointing prevarication by Glasgow's local education authority in making a small but significant shift in our nation's education system.

The college was a five-year experiment, costing just under £6.3 million over its duration, which proved to be an outstanding success. Everyone involved with the junior college assumed that if the experiment was successful, then its future could be guaranteed. However, this was not the case.

> "None of us predicted that it would be as successful as it was — and none of us predicted that this success would be declined and rejected in the way that it was and I find that appalling to be honest," says Alex Stewart, a co-founder and trustee.

The facts speak for themselves: of the 134 students, aged 14 to 16-years-old, who attended throughout its lifespan, over 75% had improved attendance records, positive post-junior college destinations in apprenticeships or on further education college courses, and the majority became advocates for the power of practical and vocationally-focused education.

> "National statistics reveal that only 75% of all 16-year-old school leavers in Scotland in 2018 gained a positive destination. Over its five years of operation 134 students attended Newlands Junior College. During the course of its five years, 19 students returned to local authority schools for a variety of reasons and it is not known whether those students went on to positive destinations or not. At the time of the college's closure, 26 students returned to local authority schools to complete their statutory education as they were not yet 16. At the time of their admission to Newlands Junior College, students' previous schools estimated that only about 25% might gain positive outcomes. Of the 89 students who completed their education

6

at Newlands, 92.1% went on to a positive destination; further education, an apprenticeship or a job. This is an outstanding achievement. If we take into account the 19 students who had some contact with NJC but returned to local authority schools, and make the assumption that they did not attain a positive outcome, then 75.9% of 108 students went onto a positive destination. This is still three times the rate of success predicted by their schools and has to be regarded as a massive success," says Gillian Hunt, who produced a report on the college's performance.[1]

The reality was personified by a delighted mother who spoke with glowing pride about her daughter who blossomed at Newlands Junior College. *"The difference in Natalie is unbelievable, she has confidence, belief in herself. She can't believe she can do what she's doing now… Newlands Junior College has given her confidence, it's shown her she can do it"*. Natalie was not the only one.

According to Jim McColl, the Scottish business figure who instigated the idea of a junior college, an agreement to back the pilot was made with the political leadership of Glasgow City Council.

"My understanding was: if the council embarked on supporting the creation of the college — and it was proven to be successful — then it would be absorbed into the education system," he says.

All the data shows the pilot was indeed highly successful, yet the council in Glasgow chose not to adopt the idea of standalone junior colleges integrated into the city's educational provision.

In January to December 2019, there were 328,000 young people aged 16 to 24 in employment in Scotland. Yet 30,000 of this age group were unemployed over that same period, an unemployment rate of 11.3% of the age range. Over the same period, there were 209,000 young Scots classed as 'economically inactive', although three-quarters of this total were in full-time education, either still at school, college or university.[2] While more young people were moving into higher education, there were still too many so-called NEET (not in education, employment and/or training).

There are three themes in this book. One is the glorious achievement and the sense of belief instilled in this cohort of Scottish young people. These students, who were turned-off and felt rejected by mainstream schooling, were able to find refuge and success at Newlands Junior College. For each one, there is an

1 Newlands Junior College 2014-2019 Report, Gillian Hunt, 2020.
2 Annual Population Survey, January 2019 to December 2019, Scottish Government, 18th March 2020.

incredible personal journey as they are given a unique opportunity to grasp the benefits of stable and normal adult life.

Then there is the tale of political expediency and the underlying ideological conflict which permeated the discussion and debate between the public sector and the private sector. Newlands Junior College was a concept driven by Jim McColl, a private sector entrepreneur, rather than conceived by Glasgow's educational professionals. It won approval and support at the highest level from the Scottish Government. Yet, at a bureaucratic council level, there was deep suspicion and prolonged hostility to an innovation which had a transformational impact on young people.

As the COVID-19 virus pandemic in 2020 and 2021 has proven, secondary education remains a hot topic, particularly when thousands of senior school pupils faced being penalised for not being able to sit exams because of the pandemic lockdown. The controversy over a decision by the Scottish Qualifications Authority (SQA) to downgrade estimated results for schools in poorer areas knocked public confidence in how fair and equitable educational provision is handled in Scotland.

Then there is the final part about the teaching and vocational staff who were prepared to take on the challenges of this project yet were left high and dry after the college's closure. Staff were even ostracised by educational professionals who must look to their consciences for the way they behaved towards fellow teaching colleagues.

In a wider sense, it is about a Scottish education system — once admired and revered — but now falling down the international league tables, that is in denial about where it is going and how it achieves its goals. It is about an unwillingness to support an innovation and a vision purely because it emanated from a high-profile business man. It smacks of powerful yet blinkered educational authorities in Scotland who did not want it to succeed because it cast doubts on their own abilities and decision-making. But it also highlights the failure of well-meaning business people to navigate the right channels and choose the correct terminology to win the valuable support of the public sector.

On a more optimistic note, perhaps this book will highlight the positive aspects and encourage other council leaders and their authorities to take up the initiative so that Scotland does not squander a unique opportunity to change many more lives. It's a story that reveals a great deal about Scotland's ambivalence about how to actually create a fairer and more inclusive society as it approaches the end of the first quarter of the 21st century.

CHAPTER ONE:
A Chronic Fall-Out At the Big School

There are critical pathways in the growth of all humans. In young people the early stages of development are in the pre-school years which can raise the life chances of a child. Policymakers around the world have turned to early intervention as a means of offsetting the impact of poverty and social deprivation. The rationale is easy to understand: if interventions can positively affect a child's cognitive and socio-emotional development in these formative years, then the chances of the child following a positive lifelong trajectory are increased.

While the pre-school years represent the greatest opportunity in determining the future of young Scots — and much was being done at a national level to increase intervention — there was a later stage which many felt required closer scrutiny and better evaluation. This was the importance of making a successful transition between primary and secondary school, during the 11 to 13 years of age. In Scotland, this was often a difficult jump to make from a single 'parent figure' primary teacher to an 'alien' environment with multiple teachers and upheaval in school after every bell to a different classroom and another subject. It was accepted that too many young people became unsettled by this move and started to disengage after shifting to the 'Big School' and starting S1.[3] While this disengagement was not restricted to those from challenging backgrounds and occurred in all social classes, it was more prevalent where there were families on lower incomes, living in poorer conditions, with generational unemployment and often few positive role models.

A number of reasons have been cited for disengagement but one that was relevant in Scotland was the frequency of bullying, a type of behaviour that is difficult to counter as those being bullied are often too fearful of speaking up about it. Often, it was better simply to stop being exposed to the bullies — and stay away from school.

Some young people who quickly fell behind in their first years at secondary school ended on a sliding slope which ultimately dropped into an abyss.

3 In this book, S1, S2, S3 and S4 represent the first four years of a comprehensive Scottish secondary school, which are compulsory. S5 and S6 are the final two years, and represent education after the age of 16.

It was part of a deeper issue that was perplexing many people in Scotland. A young person who falls into the criminal justice system and becomes a prolonged problem costs the wider community a great deal of money. John Swinney, Scotland's Deputy First Minister and Cabinet Secretary for Education and Skills, calculated that an individual falling into the criminal system can costs the Scottish justice system up to £250,000 from that first year onwards. Although it is acknowledged that the vast majority of young people in Glasgow — 96% [4] — do not become involved with offending, and those that do rarely reoffend. But how did Scottish society end up with such a protracted issue?

The debate about education in Scotland has taxed many minds since the Second World War. There was fierce pride in a primary and secondary education system which had evolved from local parish schools, culminating in the Education (Scotland) Act of 1872, delivering universal learning to every young person in Scotland between five and 13. This took the responsibility for learning out of the hands of the Church of Scotland and made it the responsibility of elected local school boards. The age of compulsory education was extended to 14 in 1901. With almost 1,000 school boards, it was decided to create 36 local education authorities [since reorganisation in 1996 there have been 32 Scottish local councils] to streamline the system and set a comprehensive system of standards. Scotland was rightly proud of its high level of numeracy and literacy and its national standing was taken seriously by politicians and the public at large. The educational guardians were varied and included the Scottish Consultative Council on the Curriculum (SCCC), later Learning and Teaching Scotland (LTS), and both the Scottish Examination Board (SEB), and Scottish Vocational Education Council (SCOTVEC), which later merged to become the Scottish Qualifications Authority (SQA) in 1997, and the teaching profession, including the General Teaching Council for Scotland (GTCS) and the influential trade unions, the Educational Institute for Scotland (EIS) and the Scottish Secondary Teachers' Association (SSTA).

The educationist[5] James Scotland, in his two-volume assessment of Scottish education, written in the late 1960s,[6] explained that an over-riding assumption of Scottish education was that "*the training of the intellect should take priority over all other facets of the pupil's personality.*"

---

4 Youth Justice Services in Glasgow, Annual Report 2015/2016. 96% of under 18s do not offend at all in the year, while 77% of offenders committed no more than one or two offences in the year. https://www.glasgow.gov.uk
5 The author has used the term educationist instead of educationalist.
6 The History of Scottish Education, James Scotland, Hodder & Stoughton, 1970.

In essence, Scotland's school system was devised to promote literacy and analytical skills, at the expense of creativity and artistic expression.

Critics claimed teachers were too concerned with imparting facts, such as capes and bays geography, and the dates of historical battles, rather than contextualising knowledge. This became enshrined in an academic system where tests and examinations were the gold standard of success. While the debate on education spawned a million viewpoints based on the personal recollection of adults who recalled their time at school, those at the chalk-face, who dealt with young people in the classroom, resented interference in their profession from those who were seen as well-meaning amateurs with no clear understanding of modern schooling or the evolving curriculum.

Teachers were attuned to the ever-changing demands in the class-room. Indeed, the General Teaching Council for Scotland was conceived during the 1960s when the post-war baby boom generation coincided with the raising of the school leaving age, firstly from 15 years of age in 1947 and to 16 by 1972. By the early 1960s, there was a chronic shortage of teachers and bulging class sizes with nearly 40 children in some infant classes. In the 1960s and 1970s, Scottish secondary education turned comprehensive, ending selective school education in much of the public sector. Previously, those who passed the 'Qually', Scotland's equivalent to the English 11 Plus exam, went off to senior secondary schools. Those who failed went to junior secondaries. Senior secondaries, such as those in the east end of Glasgow, provided a pathway of opportunity for a minority of the working-class population of the area who were allowed to attend. Some junior secondaries did an admirable job in terms of helping pupils into employment but many achieved very little. After comprehensive reorganisation, many inner city 'comprehensives' were little more than super-sized junior secondaries.

There were regular grievances by teachers over salaries and their deteriorating conditions of employment and status in society. This, in turn, led to the first teachers' strikes, called by the EIS, and the growing prestige of the General Teaching Council, which would help the expansion of the profession, setting down entry level and certification standards for teachers, and maintaining a register of qualified teachers.

Two important reports on secondary education and the comprehensive school curriculum, the Munn Report, and the Dunning Report, entitled *Assessment for All,* in 1977, attempted to set out a new curriculum which would give all pupils the opportunity to take approved Scottish Certificate of Education examinations with teachers' continuous assessment playing an increasing part in determining the result grades. A third lesser known inquiry, the Pack Report, by Professor D.C Pack, on *Truancy and Indiscipline in Schools in Scotland* made some far-reaching and prescient comments. In the UK Parliament, Glasgow Maryhill MP Jim Craigen raised the issue saying "*The prevalence of truancy in many of our schools is serious*" [7] and he added that there was a prevalence of absenteeism among teachers and "*a fair number of teachers are cracking up under the strain of teaching*".

Throughout, the 1980s and into the 1990s, the status of the teacher in society faced challenges both inside and outside the classroom. Composite classes of more than one age group and class size of more than 25 pupils became a serious issue for the EIS. While Scotland's rural and big town academies, from Dumfries, Ayr to Wick and Elgin, and the denominational schools in the urban areas,[8] were successful in turning out able young people for the post-Robbins expansion of Scottish universities, including Stirling, Dundee, Strathclyde and Heriot-Watt, there was a definite picture where too many big city comprehensive schools were unable to achieve academic success for most of their pupils. For parents, getting into the right catchment area to get their children to a suitable 'Big School' with a good academic reputation was the antidote to fee-paying private education which was dominant in Edinburgh and prevalent in Glasgow.

Meanwhile, the intervention of Conservative Prime Minister Margaret Thatcher in Scotland's unique education set alarm bells ringing in a nation that was still overwhelmingly Labour. Thatcher's 'interference' was an unwelcome and direct challenge to Scotland's school system, eventually provoking the EIS into protracted and bitter strike action lasting two years. One of the casualties was the withdrawal by teachers of support for extra-curricular activities, such as weekend sports and school trips, which had been taken for granted by Scottish parents and the authorities for many years. For years, this had been the unpaid goodwill of thousands of teachers, but this well dried up. It meant disruption to inter-school team sports and a curbing of outward bound excursions, which would have had a long-term impact on those families which could not afford to pay for the increasing private sector leisure activities and sports clubs.

---

7 Hansard, Education debate, 3 July 1978. https://hansard.parliament.uk/Commons/1978-07-03/debates.
8 A number of local authorities fund denominational (or faith) schools. These are predominantly Roman Catholic and across Scotland account for around 15% of the primary and secondary local authority funded sector. OECD Review, 2006. www.oecd.org/edu/reviews/nationalpolicies.

By the end of the 20th century, the education debate had moved on again to suit the prevailing political Labour Party dogma. A national debate on education, inspired in the early days of a new and positive Scottish Parliament, was about defining what education meant to Scotland in the new millennium. It led to the then Scottish Executive, later the Scottish Government, establishing a curriculum review in November 2003 for the three to 18-year-old range. The result was the publication in November 2004 of a significant document entitled: *A Curriculum for Excellence.*[9] This identified four key purposes which would enable Scotland's young people to become '*successful learners, confident individuals, responsible citizens and effective contributors*'. The intention of the curriculum was well-meaning: to give young people a widespread set of experiences and outcomes to equip them for the wider world. Yet, it can be argued, this has not happened in reality.

Increasingly, there were calls from industry and from business that while *A Curriculum for Excellence* was a worthy step in the right direction, the education system was still failing to equip young people for the changing demands of the workplace. There was a disconnection between what was being taught and how young people adapted to the work environment. In parallel, in schools across Scotland, teachers signalled their increasing workloads, the behavioural issues in schools and the fall-out of dealing with the social and economic problems which spilled into the learning zone.

The Scottish Government and educational employers were regularly reminded that teachers were under-valued by society with many so disillusioned that they were deserting the profession. More recently, Seamus Searson, the SSTA General Secretary, said November 2018: "*Scottish teachers have been keeping the education system afloat despite drastic financial cuts over the last ten years. Teachers have been subjected to continuous change and increasing bureaucracy whilst expectations increase when teachers and education support staff are being reduced. At the same time teachers have seen their salaries and career prospects virtually disappear*".[10]

There was further reorganisation when the Scottish Government announced the creation of Education Scotland in October 2010. This combined the responsibilities of Her Majesty's Inspectorate of Education with Learning and Teaching Scotland, and the enlarged agency, based in Livingston, established on 1 July 2011, was tasked with supporting quality and improvement in

---

9 A Curriculum for Excellence, Scottish Executive, The Curriculum Review Group, November 2004.
10 SSTA press release, 27 November2018. https://ssta.org.uk/teachers-are-scotlands-future-ssta-sub-mission-to-career-pathways-for-teachers/

teaching and learning. Council spending on primary and secondary school education across Scotland increased by 5.1 % in real terms between 2013/14 and 2018/19, from £4.1 billion to £4.3 billion. Most of this increase was attributed to the £750 million Attainment Scotland Fund, set up by the Scottish Government in 2015 to close the poverty-related attainment gap. In 2021, there are significantly more teaching staff than in 2014. There are more than 3,500 extra teachers in 2020 than in 2014, when there were 23,401 secondary teachers and 22,960 primary teachers. There are over 25,651 primary teachers and 24,077 secondary teachers, a total of 49,728 across Scotland. Along with this, the number of support staff and home-school link workers has also increased, thanks to funding from the Attainment Scotland Fund. However, what was becoming clear was more teachers was only part of the answer as staff continued to face multiple challenges and pressures in the classroom.

.....

A leading business figure, Lord Robert Smith of Kelvin, entered the debate and, on 2nd June 2011, he sent his recommendations to the Scottish Government at St Andrew's House in Edinburgh[11]. In a letter addressed to Alex Salmond, then the First Minister of Scotland, and copied to the leaders of all of Scotland's political parties, Smith clearly articulated a major challenge for Scotland which required proper attention. It also needed a broader sweep of the educational picture in the country — and the ability to tackle some unsavoury home truths.

Robert Smith was not an educationist nor part of the Scottish educational establishment. He was a successful financial and investment leader and the chairman of several organisations, including the chair of the Glasgow 2014 Commonwealth Games. He was renowned for his unfailing politeness but there was a steeliness in his resolve that he would not be pushed around or patronised by educational experts.

The Smith Group, with Smith in the chair, had been active since 2005 advising and guiding successive administrations on education policy, enterprise in education and youth employment issues. In particular, the group was focused on young people 'not in education, employment and/or training', the so-called NEET category. This report marked the culmination of the work of this group.

Smith maintained the composition of his committee was its strength. He declared that his committee had been working on the basis that there were

11 The Smith Group – Recommendations for the Scottish Government, 24 November 2011. www2.gov.scot/Publications/2011/11/SmithGroupReport

no sacred cows and were '*not beholden to any political party, ideology or policy approach.*'

The group was populated by a band of active Scottish entrepreneurs, including Sir Tom Hunter, Chris van der Kuyl, Lord Willie Haughey, and Jim McColl. They were all successful entrepreneurs in their own right and had been the nucleus of the Entrepreneurial Exchange, an organisation which has done a great deal to promote a culture of enterprise in Scotland. There was no doubt that these individuals, who had worked hard and done well in their business endeavours, wanted to make a genuine difference in their homeland. Like Smith, each one was bold enough to stand up and speak out about the state of education. Smith's note that the committee was not beholden to any political party was an important aspect of its independence.

Also on the committee were Christine Wilson, Peter Galloway, Rory Mair, then chief executive of COSLA, the organisation looking after Scotland's 32 local councils, and Julia Swan, a former teacher and chair of a NHS board in Scotland. Local authority representation was important because the provision of schooling is a statutory function of all local councils: with each authority determining its own education policies and budgets regardless of the financial contribution of central government. Teachers are employed and their salaries paid by the local authority, although pay and conditions are agreed at a national level, while the curriculum requirements are set by the Scottish Government.

The Smith Group was keen to determine the factors which contributed to a young person ending up in the NEET category and what interventions could be most effective in helping a young person find employment or training. Smith's report made pertinent points about education in Scotland and set out tangible recommendations. The committee already had a track-record as a thoughtful contributor to the education debate. It had raised a deeper understanding of the NEET issue across Scotland, working with the Scottish Government, employers, local authorities and educationists. A framework called More Choices, More Chances (MCMC) had been shaped by the Smith Group and new data and information was being captured on the school population and post-school destinations for young people. This previously unknown information helped to focus attention on what was happening to young people once they left school. When the MCMC report was launched in June 2006, it identified that 40% of the lowest attaining pupils came from 10% of the most deprived communities in Scotland.

Despite Scotland's excellent traditions of education and a steady movement towards a more highly qualified labour force, Scotland still had a higher proportion of NEETs compared to many other Organisation for Economic Co-operation and Development (OECD) countries, yet at the same time statistics showed it had the highest employment rate for 16 to 19-year-olds of OECD countries.[12]

> "Across Scotland the number of 16-19 year olds in NEET has remained fairly stable at between 1 in 7 and 1 in 8 of the cohort. The position relative to other countries places Scotland at the high end of the level of NEET with latest figures from OECD putting only Turkey and Mexico in a worse position to that in Scotland," said an OECD report.[13]

Why was this? Here definitions are important; the unemployed are defined as individuals who are without work, actively seeking employment and currently available to start work. The employed are those who work for pay, who are employees, or profit, self-employed and unpaid family workers, for at least one hour, or have a job but are temporarily not at work (through injury, illness, holiday, strike or lock-out, educational or training leave, maternity or parental leave, etc.) and have a formal attachment to their job. Such unemployment rate data did not take educational circumstances into account. Consequently, a young person counted as 'unemployed' in some OECD countries might in fact be enrolled in education. The ratio of unemployed non-students to the total age cohort was therefore a more appropriate way of reflecting youth unemployment. This is because young people who are looking for a job while still in education are usually seeking part-time or temporary work while studying, unlike those entering the labour market after leaving school. So there was a hidden element which was under-estimating the actual situation on the ground in Scotland. In 2003, just under 70% of 15 to 19-year-olds in Scotland were in education, compared with 19 other major industrial nations.

> "In most OECD countries, education policy seeks to encourage young people to complete at least upper secondary education. Since jobs on offer in the labour market require ever higher general skill levels and more flexible learning skills, persons with low attainment are often severely penalised. Differences in the ratio of unemployed non-students to the total youth population by level of educational

---

12 Education at a Glance, OECD Indicators, 2003. https://www.oecd.org/site/worldforum/33703760.pdf
13 OECD Review of the Quality and Equity of Education Outcomes in Scotland, Diagnostic Report, 2006. www.oecd.org/edu/reviews/nationalpolicies.

attainment are an indicator of the degree to which further education improves the economic opportunities of any young person," said a further OECD report.[14]

A Labour Force Survey found that an estimated 36,000 young people — or 13.2% of all 16 to 19-year-olds — were classed in the NEET category. This was a male-dominated cohort with around 5,000 classed as sick or disabled people, another 4,000 were in full-time caring roles supporting other family members. What the survey showed was that 56% of those characterised as NEET in 2003 remained NEET the following year with 21% unemployed and 35% inactive. Only 30% were moving into the workplace and even fewer, just 13%, into further education.[15] In commenting on Scotland, the OECD stated: *"persistent long term NEET status is a problem for a significant number of young people."*

The educational third sector organisation, Skill Force Scotland also estimated that this group of 36,000 young people, leaving school without a single qualification, were likely to be in the lowest-paid sectors when they eventually found work. Furthermore, a young person in the NEET category was five times more likely to have a criminal record than other sections of society.

Moreover, the cost of the NEET cohort impacted on individuals, government and society as a whole. A 2002 study by the UK's Department of Education & Skills estimated the total lifetime costs of being NEET at the age of 16 and 18 was £7 billion in future resources required [2000 figures] and £8.1 billion to the public finances, while the average per capita total over a lifetime associated with being NEET amounted in resource between £45,000 and £52,000 per annum of public finance costs, a figure which represented the costs of unemployment, crime, poor health, substance abuse, premature death and early motherhood.[16]

Furthermore, an Audit Commission report in 2009 confirmed that young men across the UK who were NEET were three times more likely to suffer from depression and prolonged mental health issues.

This was not a healthy position for Scotland's leading politicians who wanted to portray the nation as a progressive, advanced European country. The Deputy First Minister and Minister for Enterprise and Lifelong Learning was Nicol

14 Education at a Glance, OECD Indicators, 2003. www.oecd.org/site/worldforum/33703760.pdf P290.
15 OECD Review of the Quality and Equity of Education Outcomes in Scotland, Diagnostic Report, 2006. P43. www.oecd.org/edu/reviews/nationalpolicies
16 Godfrey, C., Hutton, S., Bradshaw, J., Coles, B., Craig, G. and Johnson, J. (2002). Estimating the Cost of Being 'Not in Education, Employment or Training' at Age 16-18, London: DfES.

Stephen, MSP, and Peter Peacock, Minister for Education and Young People, were well aware of the NEET problem and demanded action in parallel with Workforce Plus, and Employability Framework in Scotland.

And they understood the NEET hotspots were Glasgow, West Dunbartonshire, North and East Ayrshire, Clackmannanshire, Inverclyde and Dundee, generally in postcodes ranked in the most deprived in the Scottish Index of Multiple Deprivation (SIMD). However, Stephen and Peacock were politicians in a Scottish coalition government of Labour and Liberal Democrats and their time in office was numbered, as the Scottish National Party moved into ascendency. On Thursday, 3rd May 2007 the Scottish people, in their third devolved elections for the Scottish Parliament, increasingly favoured the SNP who created a minority government with Alex Salmond as First Minister. It was an historic moment for Scotland.

Education remained high on the political agenda. In June 2007, one of the first actions of Fiona Hyslop, the new Cabinet Secretary for Education and Lifelong Learning, was to abolish graduate endowment fees of around £2,300, a precursor to the abolition of tuition fees for university students in Scotland.

Speaking in the Scottish Parliament, Hyslop said:

> "Our country's demographic challenges over the next 20 years mean that we must make the most of the opportunities for all our people and must give everyone the chance to make the fullest possible contribution to economic and civic life. Our vision of a smarter Scotland is one in which the benefits of education are spread widely and equitably. That will be possible in the context of higher education only if access to it is driven by ability alone. For some people who have the ability to succeed, the existing structures act as barriers to their future success."[17]

Amid her answers to MSPs on this announcement was one key fact that the percentage of students from areas of multiple deprivation who were heading to university was still static, at only 12%. One MSP[18] pointed out that Jim McGoldrick, of the Scottish Funding Council, said only about 14% of people from working-class backgrounds — the same figure as 30 years earlier — get to university.

Three years later, the Smith Report was still raising the issue of NEET. Smith said: "There is now a greater appreciation of, and focus on, steering young

---

17 Scottish Parliament, speech by Fiona Hyslop, The Cabinet Secretary for Education and Lifelong Learning, 13 June 2007. www.parliament.scot/parliamentarybusiness/report.aspx-?r=4731&i=38642&c=897694&s=graduate%2520endowment
18 Alex Neil, MSP for Central Scotland, in Scottish Parliament debate, 13 June 2017.

people towards 'positive destinations' by school leaderships and education authorities."

The group also emphasised the increasing importance of 'pastoral support' for young people as they proceeded towards and started work. This would later become a voluntary movement to ensure that more pupils had mentors from similar backgrounds to encourage young people to move towards college.

While some philosophical educationists and advocates of the liberal arts and humanities speak about education as 'nutrition for the human soul', the Smith Report was more pragmatic. It was clear that the role of education and training was a means of gaining the proper skills to take a young person nearer to fulfilling employment. The Smith Group's recommendation included' introducing a system of Training Champions — a modern take on the trade system of 'journeyman' who once steered and directed apprentices on the shop floor — to motivate and inspire young people; basing examination awards on a combination of learning, not purely academic, but with training and work placement performance properly considered, and ensuring a flexible programme of learning based around useful workplace competencies.

The report advocated a central role for Skills Development Scotland (SDS) as the critical deliverer of advice to employers, young people and training providers, and recommended SDS should take control of the implementation of apprentice training across Scotland.

By 2011, Scotland was only emerging from the global banking crisis, when the economy was battered and youth employment across much of Europe was at desperately high levels. The banking collapse and the lingering recession in 2008 and 2009 turned out to be a drastic period of austerity which took its toll on younger people. More than one in six 18 to 22-year-old were unemployed in 2012, twice the rate of the rest of the working population. Leaving school education and looking for a job in a recession is tough for a young person's prospects, simply because there are fewer vacancies and companies cut back on taking on new people. The downturn was — despite output falling by more than in the early-1980s recession — less severe in terms of unemployment than previous ones. The unemployment rate in 2012 was 8%, rather than 12% in 1984 and 10% in 1993. Nevertheless, around one-in-four of the economically active people who left education in the two years to 2011 were unemployed at that point. Academic studies show that recessions are more severe for people with lower levels of formal education and there is evidence that recessions lead to other poor outcomes, such as increasing the likelihood that young people will turn to crime.[19]

While young people in the UK were more likely to find employment than in most other European nations, there was still a large number of disengaged young people without access to the world of work, and this remained an engrained problem in Glasgow and its surrounding regional council areas.

Lord Smith's view on existing secondary school provision was clear.

> "In the context of a young person being equipped to make an effective contribution to Scotland's economy, it cannot be seen as a final destination."

What the report made clear was Scotland's elected political leaders needed to concentrate on the outlook for young people leaving learning and training and attempting to find productive work in the labour market. It was the politicians' job to set the course and create the right economic environment for the creation of jobs. The cost to society of ignoring disaffected 16-19 year olds, he maintained, were enormous.

> "We recommend that the issue is of such significance that it should be tackled through a dedicated ministerial portfolio, rather than an 'add-on' to a wider brief," said Lord Smith.

A number of remedies were being considered, but the recession was particularly tough for Scotland's hard-pressed local authorities, who were under pressure as budgets and council tax increases on citizens were frozen.

> "We understand that local authorities must have the autonomy in spending decisions in order to address local priorities. The concordat between the Scottish Government and councils recognised this" he said.

The Smith Group asserted that the seriousness of the NEET situation warranted secure funding, and sought to apply business logic to this problem. They argued for a proper analysis of the destinations of young people when they left secondary education, and learning to be more aligned with the expectations of the workplace.

There was a deep-seated problem with economic inactivity a pronounced facet of the NEET cohort. The popular tabloid media spoke about a "feckless

---

19 B Bell, A Bindler & S Machin, Crime Scars: Recessions and the Making of Career Criminals, The Review of Economics and Statistics, July 2018.

young tribe" [20]of Scots who were a generation destined for hopelessness.

What was emerging was a complex picture, but linked to this was a public health crisis. In 2012, Glasgow had a notorious reputation as a city with the lowest life expectancy in Western Europe. Life expectancy at birth in Glasgow was the lowest in the UK – more than six years below the national average. Glasgow men live on average to 71.6 years, when the UK average was 78.2 years, and for women 78 years, compared to 82.3 for the rest of the UK.

Academics Walsh, McCartney, Collins and Batty in a research paper assessed 17 competing explanations for Glasgow's ill health, including poverty, vitamin D deficiency, damp and chilly winters, poor diet, a culture of "hedonism, sectarianism, and alienation", drug addiction, and the Conservative policies of Margaret Thatcher. David Walsh, a researcher at Glasgow Centre for Population Health, at Glasgow University, speaking to *The Guardian*, concluded that "the main thing to say is that it's not going to be one thing. It's going to be a combination of different factors interacting."[21]

In the same newspaper edition, Johann Lamont, then Scotland's Labour leader, and a former English teacher at Castlemilk High School and Springburn Academy, spoke about working with social workers and education psychologists largely asking: '*Why do children fall out of school?*"

> "I've got a very deep and abiding passion about education being far more than buildings and textbooks: it's what children bring into school with them. A lot of our job was drawing youngsters into school, working with families," [22] she admitted.

If you could captivate young people with the magic of learning and sustain that interest this was likely to ensure better learning outcomes that could fuel an individual's aspiration.

Then there was another element. That a young person's domestic environment was often the root cause, brought up in a home where generational unemployment was endemic and poverty had spilled into alcohol and substance abuse.

> "The group also believes that effective targeting, based on reliable evidence, supports a case for significant levels of investment in those

---

20 More choices, More chances: A strategy to Reduce the Proportion of Young People not in Education, Employment or Training in Scotland, Scottish Executive report, 2006. https://dera.ioe. ac.uk/6355/7/0030812_Redacted.pdf
21 What's wrong with Glasgow? *The Guardian*, 7th November 2012.
22 Interview: Facing up to Scotland's stark choice, *The Guardian*, 7th November 2012.

parts of Scotland where the NEET problem is highest," said Smith. Early intervention can make a profound difference to their chances in life," he said.

Among Smith's group, Tom Hunter was determined to make his mark, but there was typical inertia among swathes of the sceptical teaching profession. For example, Xlerate with XL, a programme operated jointly by the Prince's Trust Scotland and Young Enterprise Scotland (YES), was offered free to schools in Scotland, but many turned it down. Funded by Determined to Succeed and The Hunter Foundation, set up by Marion and Tom Hunter in 1998, Xlerate with XL was working to improve educational and employment outcomes for young people who are less motivated by the traditional formal curriculum.

Developed by the Prince's Trust for Scotland, Young Enterprise Scotland and the Prince's Scottish Youth Business Trust, the in-school programme worked with disaffected young people in S3 and S4 taking part over two years in a combined personal development, citizenship and enterprise course. The course, which included a 12-week enterprise module based around the YES franchise product, involved the young people in all aspects of business from product costing and business planning to manufacturing, sales plans, financial controls, training and customer satisfaction.

Involving the business community through enhanced work placements and business advice, Xlerate with XL, an option in S2, and was set to support 2,100 young people across Scotland. It never made the grade and was dropped for more positive entrepreneurial programmes.[23] Ewan Hunter, chief executive of the Hunter Foundation, said an internal evaluation by the Prince's Trust had shown that 90% of 1,800 young people involved in Xlerate with XL had gone back into education in a positive way.

> "There has been a reluctance to engage. We don't know if this is just because it's new and the evaluation has not been seen yet," he told the . *Times Educational Supplement Scotland* (TESS).

Yet it was probably ahead of its time.

What was clear was that the teaching profession and the EIS had an ingrained suspicion of 'Del-Boy' business and entrepreneurial people with ideas about the education of young people in Scotland. The upper echelons of the teaching profession persisted in pushing the brightest and, often the most

---

23 Schools 'reluctant' to xlerate with Sir Tom, TES Scotland, 28 April 2006.

fortunate, into careers in medicine, dentistry, veterinary science, the law and accountancy, professional domains where insider knowledge and nepotism, both overt and under-stated, were rife.

Teachers working in the less-privileged school environments began to embrace Opportunities for All, a banner under which all young people, between the ages of 16 and 20, would be given access to transitional training to raise their horizons and improved career options. Opportunities for All became an explicit commitment to offer a place of learning or training to every 16-19 year old classed as NEET. It was this slogan — Opportunities for All — which resonated with one of the Smith Group panel, Jim McColl.

CHAPTER TWO:
Jim McColl Steps In

Jim McColl was born in Glasgow and brought up in a working-class family in the village of Carmunnock, on the rural fringes of the city. His early years growing up and his primary school education, where rich and poorer children in the village mixed and played together, mean a great deal to him.

Today he is a successful entrepreneur who runs Clyde Blowers Capital, a private equity firm investing in global firms with engineering innovation and technological excellence at their core. He is a national public figure known for this acumen and respected in international business circles. More recently, he has been in the news over the Ferguson shipyard in Port Glasgow which he saved from administration in 2014, and was subsequently nationalised by the Scottish Government. That's another story for another place.

From modest West of Scotland beginnings, McColl understood how consistent endeavour coupled with continuing and useful learning can transform an individual's life. As a young man, he enjoyed fixing his own motor cars, completed an engineering apprenticeship at Weir Pumps in Cathcart, [in the same building that would become the Newlands Junior College] and went off to the University of Strathclyde in Glasgow, graduating with a degree in technology and business studies. He realised that those who were 'successful' in business had a deeper understanding of accounting and a greater ability to marshal their finances. While working, he furthered his studies to postgraduate level with an MBA at Strathclyde, and then an MSc in international finance at the University of Glasgow. After this, he joined an international accountancy group and became a company 'doctor'.

All this time, McColl's entrepreneurial zeal was evolving and he wanted to manage and run his own company. This opportunity came when he met with the elderly owner of Clyde Blowers, based in Clydebank. It was a long-established company with its shares publicly listed on the London Stock Exchange. The company manufactured mechanical soot-blowing products for ships, steam engines and power stations, which made boilers more efficient. It was a highly specialist and limited market. McColl took a stake in this business and saw the importance of increasing the international market share.

He invited a colleague, Bill Thomson, to join him and they set about growing

Clyde Blowers. This expansion depended on two things: buying other soot-blowing businesses and growing in China through joint venture partnerships. As China's economy expanded, so too did the demand for products that increased boiler efficiency. McColl and Thomson, joined by financial thoroughbreds, Alex Stewart and Graham Lees, were able to buy several competitive companies. In less than five years, the Clyde Blowers team consolidated their market buying up several global competitors. Their game-changing acquisition was buying the Bergemann Group, based in Germany, makers of excellent soot-blowers, in October 1996.

Moving headquarters first to Bridgeton in Glasgow and then East Kilbride, McColl and his team built a series of major companies delivering market leading products. Over time, the Clyde Blowers managers realised they had an aptitude for growing other engineering businesses too. This pushed McColl and his team in a pivotal direction and a first fund allowed Clyde Blowers to buy suitable engineering businesses with mission-critical components and after-sales service opportunities. Clyde Blowers' new role was to manage these companies on behalf of investors, which included asset managers and pension funds for teachers and lecturers.

The full entrepreneurial brilliance was seen when Clyde Blowers set up a pneumatic container system to remove drilling spoil from North Sea oil rigs. A stroke of genius – and changing regulations – helped create CleanCut Technologies, which was sold to an energy major, and remains a critical system for protecting the marine environment from the impact of the international oil industry.

Clyde Blowers' companies enjoyed major success in the United States and China and had footprints around the rest of the world. Closer to home, McColl stepped in to save the ailing Glasgow-based pump business part of Weir Group. This was another leap forward for Clyde Blowers, who were regarded as a mid-size private equity investment group. Clyde Blowers Capital made more significant acquisitions, moving into the field of renewable energy and, in particular, gears for wind turbines and into 'harmonic' components for industrial robots. While McColl's most famous intervention in his homeland was the controversial rescue of the Ferguson Marine shipyard, the last commercial ship-building yard on the River Clyde, his international career was so much more.

McColl is a devoted advocate of the power of positive thinking. His view is that nothing is impossible. And when you approach a problem, the question you ask is, '*How can we fix this?*' He is willing to keep learning and remains open-minded and frank. He sets goals for himself and his businesses and communicates clearly and regularly to those who work alongside him. He expects commitment and hard work, but he is also able to enjoy the benefits of his success, and allow others to do the same.

His friend and colleague, Alex Stewart, joined Clyde Blowers in September 1995 and his career path primed him for his 20 years of exemplary service. The Clyde Blowers' boss and the 38-year-old Ernst & Young accountant hit it off from the start. Born in Girvan, his father and mother both worked in the Royal Bank of Scotland. His father, Alexander, from a Perthshire lawyer's family, who served as a wireless operator in submarines for the duration of the Second World War, had joined the bank, meeting his mother, Mary, a local Ayrshire lass. Alex junior was only 11 months when his father was seconded to Lombard Street, to work for the Royal Bank in the London head office. His first 11 years were spent in England, growing up in central London and then Bishop's Stortford in the Home Counties, before the family returned in 1969. He entered Airdrie Academy at 11, and with a soft English accent, supporting Tottenham Hotspur, and survived, thrived and excelled at maths and science, including chemistry, and went to university, aged 16.

He considered becoming a surgeon, but his father wanted him to pursue a career in law, like his grandfather in Perthshire. Young Alex was taken to meet Professor David Walker, the doyen of Scots Law and Dean of the Faculty of Law and Financial Studies at the University of Glasgow. He stood his ground and, as a compromise, in 1975, Stewart enrolled to undertake a Bachelor of Accountancy degree, which was in the law faculty at Gilmorehill. This was a new academic approach moving away from indentured accountants' training on the job in existing offices. After graduation, he joined Whinney Murray, at 175 West George Street in Glasgow, which would evolve through to Ernst & Whinney, merging with Arthur Young to eventually become Ernst & Young. As a trainee, he progressed towards becoming a fully qualified member of the Institute of Chartered Accountants in Scotland (ICAS), qualifying as a CA in 1981.

McColl and Stewart enjoyed immense international business success working together and Stewart was always a reliable sounding board for McColl's business ideas. When McColl first raised the issue of setting up a junior college to tackle the issue of NEETs and help young people excluded from school, Stewart's natural reluctance, as a corporate accountant, was that they should leave education to the professionals. And while they shared a set of values which understood the power of useful education and practical learning to change and enrich lives, Stewart was unconvinced by a college as the solution. However, they were Scots who abhorred the waste of talent and genuinely wanted to use the fruits of their labour to do something important. This was at the heart of their commitment to Newlands Junior College and to its students and former students. Stewart, the original reluctant supporter, would change his mind and become one of the College's most ardent mentors, supporters and individual funders.

CHAPTER THREE:
A Stubborn Problem Needs a Fix

Even in 2021, Scotland still faces a lingering problem that has not gone away and it is linked with education — this is the level of national productivity. This issue is likely to be exacerbated by the shock of the COVID-19 pandemic, which has claimed millions of lives around the world and wrecked international economies, and the impact of the United Kingdom eventually leaving the European Union in January 2021.

Speaking before the corona virus outbreak, Tracy Black, the director of Confederation of British Industry (CBI) Scotland and a board member of Skills Development Scotland in launching a new annual productivity index along with KPMG [24], said:

> "We all know that Scotland faces a productivity challenge, with recent weaknesses highlighting the need to find new solutions that can deliver a real step-change. ... Brexit aside, boosting productivity has been the number one priority for CBI Scotland over the past couple of years. For us, this isn't just some academic exercise, we're absolutely determined to find real world solutions to a stubborn problem that can deliver more jobs, higher wages and future prosperity across the whole country."

On average, it took a Scottish worker a five-day working week to produce the same item that took only four days in the Netherlands, and less compared with the Far East and China. But productivity had been a stubborn issue which businesses in the UK and in Scotland had been poring over for a decade or more. While productivity is linked to the levels of investment in equipment, machinery and emerging technologies, it is also related to the skills and knowledge of the workforce.

In August 2008, a report from the Recruitment & Employment Confederation, a not-for-profit membership organisation for the recruitment industry, showed that 92% of recruiters rated the performance of school leavers as 'average' or 'below average'.

---

24 Productivity progress but Scotland starts a lap behind the competition: CBI Scotland and KPMG report, 9 September 2019. www.cbi.org.uk/media-centre/articles/productivity-progress-but-scotland-starts-a-lap-behind-the-competition/

More than half (56%) did not think the basic literacy and numeracy skills of school leavers was up to scratch. Almost three-quarters (73%) did not think recruits from schools had the proper attitude about going to work. The majority of respondents (82%) believed the UK education system was failing to prepare students with the relevant skills for the workplace. Unrealistic expectations coupled with a poor work ethic was the main cause of concern according to 73% of recruiters. Of course, this was hardly an academic study but it raised the thorny issue of how well prepared — or otherwise — the Facebook generation was for the employment market.

Then Sir Stuart Rose, speaking at the CBI conference in November 2009, expressed his extreme concern about the huge gap between the best and worst-qualified school leavers. The then chairman of retail giant M&S, said: *"We have to worry about those people who don't have the 21st century equivalent of metal-bashing, whether that is computer literacy or something else. They are not fit for work when they come out of college,"* he maintained.

His comments resonated with Chris Hyman, chief executive of Serco, a public services outsourcing company, who said that the British education sector was failing the economy by not producing the right kind of graduates.

Richard Lambert, then the CBI director and the former *Financial Times* editor, said the priority for the political parties campaigning for the UK General Election in 2010, should be addressing the huge number of young people leaving school without qualifications.

Then, in 2011, Scottish Investment Operations, a professional body for the financial sector, including fund and pension fund management, highlighted there was a growing problem with graduates who were ill-equipped for the workplace. The research, involving over 20 key financial service companies in Scotland, including Barclays, Clydesdale Bank [now Virgin Money], Royal Bank of Scotland, and Tesco Bank, found that candidates were unable to articulate themselves well and could not be relied upon to communicate with customers and colleagues effectively without additional training. Written communication, important when sending out information to customers, was also poor in terms of grammar, sentence construction and basic spelling errors.

Moreover, SIO pointed out school leavers and graduates were failing to understand what a job in financial services entailed, leading to negative perceptions of a vital industry for the country. This encouraged SIO to reposition itself as an organisation with three strategic priorities, two of which were promoting the industry and developing the skills of the workforce. Vida Rudkin, chair of SIO Forum and a managing director of Morgan Stanley in Glasgow, said: *"Everything comes down to our people. We need to ensure we have the right people and the right skills in the right location and always plan for the future i.e. attract the right people and give them options to meet their expectations"* [25].

There remained genuine concerns for Scotland's economic future considering the finance and banking sector was responsible for employing one in ten Scots at the time, around 90,000 people, and accounted for 7% of the GDP.

It was not only the financial services sector where school leavers were lacking in vital skills, the same issue also resonated with Eddie Hawthorne, the chief executive of Arnold Clark, the Glasgow-headquartered motor dealership which was one of the largest private companies in Scotland. Hawthorne would play an important role in the Newlands Junior College story, becoming an original trustee.

An Engineering and Technology skills survey in 2010 flagged the difficulty. Employers were planning to recruit new staff, yet many were struggling to find suitable candidates, with 21% finding it hard to find appropriate engineering graduates.

Over the following decade, a broad consensus emerged across many sectors in Scotland that the school system was failing to produce enough suitably qualified candidates for industry and commerce. Moreover, too many were unable to take advantage of career opportunities in the emerging new technologically-based workplaces, and the disruptive world of Industry 4.0, where 'meta-skills' of critical thinking, problem solving and creativity were highly prized in driving innovation. It was a wake-up call which resulted in Skills Development Scotland, now the national state-run skills agency, tasked with working with Education Scotland and schools to support all young people to 'My World of Work', a portal where young people could build their CV and seek work experience opportunities from S3. The organisation stated one of its ambitions was to support Scotland in taking its place among the top-ranking OECD countries for productivity.[26]

In 2021, a report from Audit Scotland entitled *Improving Outcomes for Young People Through School Education* spoke about attainment being more than

25 SIO, Scottish Investment Operations, 28 August 2016, www.sio.org.uk/news/sourcing-and-managing-talent-blog
26 Skills Development Scotland. Strategy Plan 2019-2022. www.skillsdevelopmentscotland.co.uk/media/45753/a-human-future-strategic-plan-2019-2022.pdf

'just exam results'. School education "also aims to improve children's and young people's health and wellbeing and support wider outcomes such as vocational qualification." The report spoke about the importance of different pathways and opportunities but said there was a wide variation in education performance across councils, "with evidence of worsening performance on some indicators in some councils."

The report pointed out that council spending on primary and secondary school education across Scotland increased by 5.1% between 2013 and 2019 to £4.3 billion, much of this attributed to the £750 million Attainment Scotland Fund, set up to close the poverty-related attainment gap. One of the findings was the way the Attainment Fund was targeted "does not fully capture pupils living in poverty." Indeed, gaining access to this financial support was an issue for Newlands Junior College.

Rightly or wrongly, a large part of the lingering problem about national productivity was laid at the door of Scotland's secondary schools, where too many young people were becoming disengaged with education long before they were leaving school for the work environment. More recently, another factor has emerged: the unprecedented disruption caused by the COVID-19 pandemic, with school shut-downs and businesses locked down, has drastically curtailed work experience opportunities. This was still being felt as this book was published, but it was obvious that this too would become a further hindrance for disadvantaged young people looking for useful employment.

CHAPTER FOUR:
The Genesis of A Junior College Takes Shape

Dr Bill Gerrard was the training officer for Weir Pumps, the multinational engineering business founded in Cathcart, which made industrial pumps and their control systems for international customers in minerals, defence, the oil and gas and the water industries. With more than a touch of personal sentiment, Jim McColl stepped in to buy the Cathcart division of Weir Group in May 2007. Shortly after, his company, Clyde Blowers Capital, concluded an audacious deal with Textron in the United States to buy its subsidiary Union Pumps, merging it with its Weir division, to the create an enlarged CLYDEUNION Pumps.

As an engineer to trade, Gerrard became head of the CLYDEUNION Academy, established by Jim McColl in May 2008, and officially opened by Glasgow's Lord Provost Bob Winter, and with connection to Glasgow Caledonian University, which set up training courses for engineers and partnerships with academic institutions across Scotland and overseas. The academy embraced the latest teaching technology of the time, including the use of white interactive SMART boards.

As part of his remit, Dr Gerrard was asked by Jim McColl in 2010 to look into why a small, but significant, group of young people were disengaging with their secondary school education.

To be clear, this was not a problem unique to Scotland. Across the rest of the UK and in the United States, it was an endemic issue. However, the New York City's Department of Education District 79 Alternative Schools Program was a testament to what could be achieved. District 79 was a citywide network of over 300 alternative schools and programmes serving the City's most needy students. In all, 21,000 young people and 50,000 adults who were some distance away from a high school diploma were being pulled back into the education system. District 79 was designed to help disengaged young people get academic instruction along with new opportunities.

> "We recognise that many students need additional supports to succeed in their current school or require alternative pathways to attain a high school or General Education Diploma (GED) diploma. District 79

was established to help students succeed by providing diverse and innovative educational opportunities that combine rigorous academic instruction with meaningful youth development," stated its aim.

The vision remained that every student in District 79 will succeed academically while developing socially and emotionally to become a confident and productive member of society.

Gerrard, who was inspired by the New York District 79 programme, said in his preliminary report:

"It is recognised by educationalists that many students would need additional support to succeed in their current school environment, the provision of which is not always available nor feasible. It is also widely felt that students who are disengaged from school work may require alternative pathways to re-engage and attain their full potential."

Gerrard summed up this 'alternative pathway' in a single sentence.

"It is proposed to create an alternative approach which will combine diverse and innovative vocationally-oriented educational opportunities with rigorous academic instruction and meaningful youth development." [27]

At its core, this approach had to make those arriving in a new place of education feel that they had an attachment with the place. This was about a 'sense of belonging' and Gerrard quoted *Webster's New Collegiate Dictionary* to find the definition "*to belong*". It was "*to have a proper, appropriate, or suitable place. To be naturally associated with something. To fit in a group naturally.*"

"Indeed, conventional practices may exacerbate feelings of rejection and alienation and place these students at higher risk of dropping out, joining gangs or using drugs," he said.

Teachers in mainstream schools work to assimilate a set of positive values related to respect, pride and involvement, but the teacher-student relationship has been under increasing stress because of classroom sizes, behavioural disruption, and examination workloads, while the constant shifting of pupils after a single or double period of teaching to another classroom meant many were failing to cope with the organisational upheaval.

Of course, the majority of students in mainstream Scottish education can and

---

27 Preliminary Investigation into Development of Newlands Junior College, Bill Gerrard, 11 February 2011.

do build a sense of belonging and pride in their school through their involvement with both curricular and non-curricular activities, such as sport, dance, music and drama. This involves open and healthy relationships between teachers and students and creates value in most of Scotland's schools. What is now better understood is that each child matures at a different age and in a different way. But among at-risk students, who felt anonymous and lonely in larger school environments, the conventional Scottish classroom experience was failing to engender any sense of belonging. The school experience had nothing to offer them and they felt alienated by classmates and teachers. This often resulted in bullying. Very quickly, this group of students can withdraw from mainstream school life and become disaffected and disengaged. Moreover, a minority become disruptive, unruly and exerted negative influences on other students. This was a toxic spiral which had consequences for both school pupils who wanted to learn and engage and those who did not.

Gerrard's initial report was welcomed by Jim McColl, who asked his colleague Alex Stewart to help develop this thinking. Stewart, who was approaching retirement from Clyde Blowers, began devoting some of his time and energy to what he later admitted was one of the crowning achievements of his life.

> "I have to say to my shame, I said to Jim, 'This is not our job. We have other day jobs to do. It's not for us. What do we know about education? We're not trained in this field'. I refused to get involved on at least two formal occasions," he recalls. [28]

Gradually, Stewart was reeled into the next stages of the creation of Newlands. As part of the process, a limited company was incorporated on 23rd August 2011, but it remained dormant until trading began in May 2014, and it was then registered as a charity regulated by OSCR (Office of the Scottish Charity Regulator).

> "Before I was involved with the college, Jim McColl was involved in a number of committees with local government and the Scottish Government. It was all about Back to Work and Not in Education, Employment or Training. He would tell me about much of this and it sounded very interesting," he says.

Alex Stewart was pestered again by McColl to help with the development.

> "Ideally, the whole idea could have been aimed at primary school level intervention and that was proven later when we opened the college

---

28 Interview with Alex Stewart by the author, 2019.

because the average reading age of those who arrived with us was between seven and nine-years-old, even although they were young adults of 14. So the literacy issue should have been evident in primary school," says Stewart.

Gerrard's original proposals outlined a model curriculum for 14 to 16-year-olds (young people in S3 and S4) but this needed amendment with more detail about its three main strands of academic learning, vocational training and personal and physical development and wellbeing. His thoughts were refined in *The Newlands Junior College Report: An Alternative Approach for Reclaiming those Dis-engaged from Secondary School*, written in August 2012.

There were local examples of similar projects which McColl had witnessed. In August 2004, a small independent school was set up in Johnstone, Renfrewshire called Johnstone Technical Education Centre (JTEC). The premise was to act as a training wing for a local construction company, MPS Construction Limited, formerly Maxwellton Property Services, enrolling young people nearing the end of their compulsory education and offering them additional support and pre-vocational learning opportunities, working towards an apprenticeship within the construction industry. This model provided the young people with core skills, personal development, health and wellbeing and pre-vocational learning opportunities such as woodwork, constructions skills and glazing.

Within a few years the curriculum and school building grew substantially with young people attending JTEC on a full-time basis as an alternative to their 3rd and 4th years (S3 and S4) of secondary education. In 2006, two new schools were opened, the Clydebank Technical Education Training Centre (CTEC) in Clydebank and Greenock Technical Education Training Centre (GTEC) in Greenock offering similar day education placements in those local authority areas. In 2007, Jim McColl, whose company, Clyde Blowers, had been based in Clydebank for nearly 50 years, had been invited to open the Clydebank Technical Education Training Centre and was deeply impressed with what he saw. The three schools were combined in 2011 and based at the Clydebank site. Martyn Cosh, a director of MPS Construction who became head of education at CTEC, was keen to collaborate with the new junior college on the south side of Glasgow.

In 2012, CTEC received an exceptional school inspection and viewed as an exemplar in the West of Scotland. In June 2014, the school changed ownership and appointed a new board of directors, including Professor Ross Deuchar, assistant dean of the School of Education at the University of the West of Scotland, as a non-executive director. A decision was made to relocate the school to Paisley, in Renfrewshire, where it was given a new name: Mirren Park School.

The founding figures of Newlands Junior College were also considering other models and the work of the Kibble Education and Care Centre also in Paisley caught the eye. Elizabeth Kibble, a Scottish textile heiress, provided for the foundation of a charitable institution in a trust deed in 1840, known as The Kibble School, which opened its doors in 1859. The trustees were granted extensive powers to employ professional staff to carry out the school's operation. In 1995, following the imminent withdrawal of all government support for independent schools, the trustees formed the Kibble Education and Care Centre, with objectives similar to the trust, to retain the ownership of the property and policies of the school. The company's object is to carry on in Paisley or elsewhere an institution to provide for the education and care of young people who have been young offenders against the law. The place of operation is Goudie Street in Paisley and the mission is to provide a stable, purposeful, safe and happy environment for young people in trouble.

The founders looked at what was happening furth of Scotland where other nations, such as Norway, Australia and New Zealand, were running privately -funded education projects aimed at helping young people find worthwhile employment. Scottish educationists often look admiringly at the Nordic nations as an example of how a genuine comprehensive education system is delivered. Yet in Sweden, one of the most successful technological nations in the world, there was the ABB Industrigymnasium, with three schools in Vasteras, Sala and Ludvika. These were upper secondary schools focusing on engineering, information technology and enterprise set up by one of the country's major engineering firms, ABB. When Swiss Brown Boveri Corporation merged with the Swedish company ASEA, they were keen to grow the next generation of engineers. The original Ludvika school was founded by ABB in 1994 and has since been a successful route for Sweden's entrepreneurial and technology prowess. In Sweden, these independent schools, which were selective in encouraging those with good mathematics and science skills, were among the most successful and involved with Young Enterprise, a national body encouraging start-ups.

One serious option considered by Gerrard's report was basing the junior college in one of Glasgow's existing further education colleges, which were all undergoing radical transformation in the city. The City of Glasgow College was formed as a result of a merger of the Nautical College, the College of Food Technology and the College of Printing, while Glasgow Clyde College was a merger of Cardonald, Langside and Anniesland Colleges. One perceived advantage was that a junior college within an existing FE college could allow a successful pilot to be scaled up across Scotland, and this would negate the requirement to renovate the Minto Building at Cathcart, by now owned by SPX Flow, who took it over after the sale of CLYDEUNION Pumps.

However, Cardonald said it did not have the space, while the City of Glasgow College, which was undergoing a massive multi-million pound combined building project in Cathedral Street, was managing a flitting of staff and facilities over the coming years. The City of Glasgow College, and its Principal, Paul Little, would become strong supporters of the students at Newlands.

The Gerrard report, proposing different options, was sent out to interested parties to whet their appetites. It recommended using the Minto Building which adjoined the SPX Flow facility and where Jim McColl has once been an apprentice.

"I remember Jim saying to me, 'It doesn't look like anyone else is going to run with this — it looks like we'll have to do this ourselves. What Jim meant by 'ourselves' was a mixture of private industry and the Scottish business sector. Those were the people willing to help with jobs and give young people work experience," recalls Alex Stewart.

The stumbling block was not the physical building itself but how it could be transformed as a place of learning. Gerrard's report said the proposed learning environment needed to foster new ways of teaching and learning.

"While the physical arrangements can, in theory, be provided within any new or existing building, the wider context of these facilities is in itself critical," said Gerrard's report.

The Minto Building had a unique advantage: it adjoined the major engineering facility site where the sights and sounds of heavy mechanical and manufacturing activity could be seen and heard. It was visibly and aurally connected with the world of work, and not viewed purely as an educational institution.

"It is inherently something 'other'. It has the opportunity of freeing its staff and students from all the connotations of the system that, fairly or unfairly, has made them feel that they do not belong," stated Dr Gerrard in his report.

The report concluded that a stand-alone facility in the Minto Building was the best way of providing young people with a new form of secondary education in S3 and S4, preparing them for either an apprenticeship or a place in further education.

While Stewart and the trustees admired vocational college teaching, they were left in no doubt that the junior college required a group of Scottish-trained and qualified secondary teachers.

"We had to recruit fully-qualified, fully-responsible teachers, that was a given. But the real secret was to find teachers who had a particular strength or gift in working with young people where the system was saying we can't educate these people," says Stewart.

Gerrard summed it up succinctly:

"The Newlands Junior College approach should not be viewed as inferior to traditional school education but more as an additional resource offering a different approach for those who learn in different ways."

This amply set the direction for future discussion.

CHAPTER FIVE

A Colourful Dinner with Head Teachers

Jim McColl was now actively exploring the notion of starting a junior college. He wanted to float the idea with head teachers in Glasgow, so he asked permission to approach them. This was granted and, in September 2011, a gathering was invited for a good dinner and a few glasses of wine at a private venue on the outskirts of the city.

Carnbooth House, near Busby, was an elegantly-restored grade B listed hotel with original features set within eight acres of grounds five miles from Glasgow City Centre. It was a friendly and private place to have a decent supper and some open conversations. In typical fashion, McColl had prepared a brief presentation which he planned to deliver before everyone started their meal, yet there were several missing invitees. McColl pressed on and was surprised that a few head teachers were late, with one turning up 45 minutes after the start. McColl heard no apologies as the late-comer took his place at the end of the table.

That evening Iain White, the head teacher at Govan High School, sat next to Bill Gerrard. The round-the-table discussion was indeed frank and forthright but not unduly frosty.

> "We're very good at this kind of thing. We're the educators. So Jim, why don't you just give us the money and let us get on with it," said one of the heads.

> "Actually, all the data shows you're not very good at this and that's why I think we need a different approach," replied McColl.

> "What data are you using?" asked another.

> "The Scottish Government's own statistics about those who are leaving school without a positive destination," he answered.

There were plenty of questions, some decidedly tetchy, and then White raised his hand to speak.

> "Jim, how many places did you say you had at this college you're going to start?"

"We think that the maximum will be around 20 to begin with, increasing to around 30," said the businessman.

"Brilliant. Let me know when it starts and I'll send you 20 from Govan High."

This was a seminal moment for McColl's idea. Of all the head teachers in attendance, White was by far the most positive. That response made a lasting impression on McColl who was genuinely pleased that his concept had, at least, some serious educational support in Glasgow. The dinner drew to a close and the teachers all headed off.

......

Iain White's reputation as a maverick educationist extended way beyond the famed Baillieston lights on the boundary of the city of Glasgow. His name was mentioned in dispatches in educational circles in Edinburgh. He was credited with instigating the employability programme in secondary schools. The 'Govan Heidie' became a regular speaker on the conference circuit.

White's strategy for Govan High School was engagement with the local community around the school, and this included businesses on the doorstep where future opportunities for pupils would be most prevalent. Govan High took out a membership in the Southside Business Club, a not-for-profit organisation for businesses under the auspices of the Govan Initiative. This evolved into the Glasgow Business Club, with one of the teachers a conduit for meetings. The school even managed to reach the final of a local Business of the Year competition. The Govan Initiative was being run by Ron Culley and then Damien Yeates, who went on to lead Skills Development Scotland, and they were in the vanguard of the creation of Modern Apprenticeship programmes. Govan High School also achieved Investors in People accreditation.

White put himself about and was a prominent local figure, and even attended several sessions during the planning stages of the new Southern General Hospital, one of the most significant NHS projects in Scotland and re-named as the Queen Elizabeth University Hospital. This was Scotland's largest hospital, with over 1,600 acute hospital beds, a children's hospital, and a major accident and emergency department for the city, being built in the catchment area of his school.

One early session at the hospital in Linthouse was a discussion around careers in the NHS Glasgow and while all the head teachers in the south side of Glasgow were invited, White was the only one who turned up. From this, he gleaned a lot of information about the type of non-medical jobs that were required. He found this eye-opening. Outwith the qualified consultants, doctors and nurses, there were 12 allied professions, such as physiotherapists, podiatrists and radiographers, and there were more than 350 types of job in this massive new hospital complex.

It was clear there were opportunities for school leavers to undertake apprenticeships in various trades.

White also became involved with the Welfare to Work programme, which was chaired by Jim McColl, and he arranged a group breakfast meeting at the school. McColl was intrigued to visit and promised White he would return. Instead of a prize-giving, Govan High undertook 'The Oscars', where all kinds of achievement was recognised with skills development and employability rewarded rather than academic awards. There was usually a cabaret provided by music department students and then a keynote address from a guest speaker. In spring 2006, Jim McColl was proposed as the guest.

> "By this time, Jim was understanding more about these young people who were going down the stank," recalls White "So I phoned Angela Meikle, Jim's executive assistant, not because I knew her, but I thought I'd give it a shout. So I asked if Jim would come to do the keynote address. I said we could shift the date around to suit his availability." [29]

Within minutes, it was confirmed that McColl was free and could make 'The Oscars' as the speaker. *"He would love to do it. He's never been asked to do anything like this before,"* replied Meikle.

In preparation, McColl wanted to spend time in the school and was invited to come along on his way to his East Kilbride HQ. He was introduced to a mixed group of pupils and White left them together returning half an hour later after they had spoken. McColl was rapt and stayed for nearly an hour and half with the group, and later returned for the school's Oscars.

......

A few days after the Carnbooth House head teachers' dinner, White received a phone call from Bill Gerrard, who was working on an advisory basis. Gerrard had advised McColl that he really needed someone with deep experience of secondary schooling in Glasgow to develop the thinking.

---

29 Interview with Iain White by the author, June 2019.

After White's enthusiastic show of support, they agreed he was a key candidate but had to clear the approach with Maureen McKenna, the Executive Director of Education at Glasgow City Council. McKenna, a graduate of the University of Glasgow, started her teaching career in the former Grampian Region, where she taught mathematics in three secondary schools before moving back to Strathclyde and becoming principal teacher of mathematics and then assistant head teacher in Kilsyth Academy.

In 2000, she joined Her Majesty's Inspectorate of Education (HMIE), where she inspected schools as well as education authorities and handled child protection matters. McKenna held several posts within HMIE, including national specialist for mathematics and district inspector for Glasgow and North Ayrshire. She was also President of the Association of Directors of Education in Scotland (ADES). According to the *Evening Times*, her salary in April 2020 was £138,326, making her one of the top five earners in Glasgow City Council.

She joined Glasgow City Council in December 2007 as deputy to Margaret Doran, Director of Children and Families, the combined department of education and social work services, the successor to Ronnie O'Connor as Director of Education. Doran stepped down 'unexpectedly'[30] citing 'financial challenges' in August 2009, and McKenna stepped up. In 2011, McKenna agreed to a request to make the appointment of a secondment for three months to work on the junior college project.

Gerrard was able to make a serious offer.

> "So the idea is that I walk away from Govan High School and leave it for three months, and then I come back?" asked White.

> "That's it in a nutshell," said Gerrard.

> "Naw, I don't think so."

> "What do you mean?"

> "My responsibilities are to the young people who are here at the moment, so I don't fancy it."

> "Aye, but Jim McColl wants you to do it."

> "Last time I checked you worked for Jim McColl but I don't."

Several days later, White received a call from Maureen McKenna's secretary

---

30 Glasgow's schools chief quits over finance 'challenges', The Herald, 20 August 2009.

asking him to go in and speak with the Director of Education about "*this Jim McColl thing*".

The director said she could not make him do the secondment, but she would like him to undertake it as he was "*the best person for the job*". White's initial response was he did not really fancy it, although he was persuaded to talk with one of McKenna's education department deputies. According to White's recollection, the director said: "*I can't be seen not to be supportive of this, politically.*"

Meanwhile White's interest was piqued, his resistance softened and he asked Gerrard and McKenna what the task entailed. The Govan head was asked to prepare two separate papers: one on the junior college's structure and how it would be set up, and how much it would cost, with a detailed financial spreadsheet. White cited a way of working from his time in the shipyards as a student. This was a 'job-and-finish' basis, when the yard bosses needed something cleared out and tidied perfectly. The workers would be paid until 10pm, but if they finished the work by 6pm and it was spotless, they could go home. White prepared the papers on this basis and was given a desk, chair and a laptop with an internet connection. He would crack on and, as soon as it was done, he would return to Govan High. Meantime, his colleague, Philip Graham, who was acting deputy head teacher, was handed extra remits and now had a full plate, as his main focus was trying to turn the school over to its Skills Focus curriculum.

White started on Monday, 26th September 2011 and set about his task with eagerness. With room to concentrate on a single project, rather than the usual multi-tasking of a head teacher, it took him four weeks and two days. He finished both reports on Friday 4th November 2011 and headed back to Govan High the following Monday. It would be some time before he received a call from Jim McColl.

CHAPTER SIX:
Sage Advice: The Arrival of Keir Bloomer

Turning McColl's good idea into reality required someone with a deeper knowledge of how to navigate the minefield of educational policy in Scotland. Keir Bloomer was an educationist and the retired chief executive of one of Scotland's 32 regional councils. Many years earlier, he had been a history teacher in Castlemilk before rising in the educational ranks to become a senior government adviser and one of the key influencers in the creation of the Curriculum for Excellence. Furthermore, he was a passionate advocate for the reform of education in Scotland where he recognised the country was falling behind in levels of attainment. He is also convener of the Royal Society of Edinburgh's education committee.

It was shortly after the Carnbooth head teachers' dinner in Busby that Bloomer became aware of McColl's intentions. During the summer of 2012, McColl was given the name of Keir Bloomer and they met and had a customary cup of tea and a chat. Bloomer's initial question was a simple one: *What kind of educational entity would Newlands become?*

There was a limited number of possible answers with the most obvious the creation of an independent school or college. In Edinburgh, the idea of private fee-paying schools is part of the educational tapestry of the city. From Fettes College to George Watson's and George Heriot's, the panoply of choice is well understood by well-to-do people.

> "When I suggested that to Jim, he was not initially keen on this, because his picture of an independent school was Hutchie Grammar or George Watson's, or something like that. This was very much not the kind of thing he had in mind," recalls Bloomer. [31]

Bloomer reminded him that a large independent category in Scotland was the 'special schools', for many young people with special educational and emotional needs.

> "In a way, his intended school fell into that category," he says.

McColl asked Bloomer for his help in setting the wheels in motion and, imperceptibly, the college's mission began to beguile this seasoned educational

---

31 Interview with Keir Bloomer by the author, September 2019.

professional. He became a complete convert.

In order to open an independent school, there is a process of registration with the Learning Directorate of the Scottish Government, where a civil servant has the task of being the Registrar of Independent Schools. Bloomer undertook the process of obtaining the registration for Newlands Junior College.

It was a simple job to set up the registration and arrange two inspections by HM Inspectors, the first before the college could take students in and then six months after the college had been created. The first visit was to ensure the premises were satisfactory. The initial pre-registration inspection in August 2014 was undertaken by a former colleague of Bloomer who knew the former government adviser would be more than able to meet the criteria. The official inspection, in September 2015, was about ensuring proper educational provision, which had been defined by the junior college and had to fit in with national teaching standards.

Dr Bloomer, who is an honorary doctor of Queen Margaret University, outside Edinburgh, was never a junior college employee or a trustee yet he remained a paid educational consultant and undertook a range of jobs. He attended almost all of the external educational meetings over the five years. In this capacity, he attended meetings with Scottish Government officials in the Learning Directorate at Victoria Quay in Edinburgh, where the proposed college was given some prominence.

> "Jim McColl made good progress with the Scottish Government really on the back of his relationship with John Swinney, which dated back to the time when Swinney was the Finance Minister and Jim was on the Council of Economic Advisers. He already had a strong and friendly relationship with him and he found a ready audience for his ideas," says Bloomer.

Swinney's enthusiasm initially carried a great deal of weight and this was fundamental for the junior college's progression from concept to reality. The Scottish Government had stated its commitment of closing the poverty-related attainment gap in order to make the country a fairer society. This was also the mission of Newlands Junior College and, with the Minister firmly on side, there were no serious difficulties with senior civil servants in Edinburgh.

> "I never met the Minister in this connection, although I have in other matters, all my dealings were with senior civil servants and they were all aware of the fact that the ministerial wish was to make this happen," he continues.

This gave the college a clear path to its foundation. The governance structure was the creation of a charity in Scotland, set up on 30th September 2014, which would then have a board of trustees overseeing and managing the college, with McColl as chairman, Stewart as deputy chair, and any major donors, either business or local authorities, represented on the board. Allan Dowie, one of McColl and Stewart's colleagues, took on the role of Treasurer, and became a trustee along with lawyer Graeme Bruce, of CMS Cameron McKenna, Andrew Neilson, of Weir Group plc, Eddie Hawthorne, of Arnold Clark, Douglas O'Neill, of Scottish Gas, and Scott Black, of FWB Park Brown.

The Scottish Government's support was greatly encouraging for the chairman and the trustees.

> "I can say that John Swinney and his team inside the Scottish Government went above and beyond what we would have expected. They were always happy to match the money which was put in by the local authority. They had to find a proper way of doing this through their system of grants, because it is the local authorities responsibility to fund education," says Jim McColl.

In a wider sense, the funding was academic because McColl and his funders were determined to bridge the funding, which was what they did throughout the five-year pilot.

Later on, John Swinney was a welcome guest during an official visit to Newlands speaking with many of present students, including Jack, Damian, Reece, Anton, Marci, Toni and Aimee, and former students, including Jamie and Megan, who described her college experience to the Minister as "unbelievable".

The experience with Glasgow City Council was a very different kettle of fish. As an international businessman running several major companies, McColl admits he did not fully understand the nuances and machinations of how local government worked in Scotland. This proved to be an Achilles' heel for the project. He was unclear of the different executive roles and indeed the 'silos' of the various leaders within local government.

Initially, McColl had broached the subject with Steven Purcell, the charismatic council leader who represented Drumchapel and Anniesland. Purcell, as convenor of education, embraced McColl's idea and promoted it in the council, but his tenure controversially came to an end in March 2010. McColl met Purcell's successor, Gordon Matheson, who became the Labour leader of

Glasgow Council for five years from 2010 until 2015. Matheson took some interest but was never a true champion in the way Swinney and Purcell were. Politically, Matheson was prepared to go along with the concept and agreed to find a £100,000 a year grant from Glasgow's budgets for the pilot scheme.

The council had more pressing mainstream issues with a long-running claim for equal pay for council workers, while the Educational Institute of Scotland was arguing for more money and better conditions for teachers. The teaching unions began to learn more about the idea and were reluctant to give the Newlands College their full blessing when their fight was for all of the secondary school teachers in Glasgow. In the longer run, this would mean a wage settlement for teachers that further squeezed any prospect of alternative educational innovation in cash-straitened councils.

Furthermore, the relationship with Maureen McKenna was a nervous one. She was in a very powerful position controlling an annual expenditure of £598 million in 2020 figures, which was two in every five pounds of the city's £1.58 billion annual expenditure. The bulk of this was for teachers' pay, which was £154 million for Primary Teachers, and £133 million for Secondary Teachers, and £79 million for Early Years employee costs. Additional support for learning was another £65 million, with third party payments of £6.5 million. The irony was that £1.29 billion of the total came from central government with only £290 million raised from local council taxes in Glasgow. Certainly, the Education Department was omnipotent but it was also duty-bound to listen to the political paymasters in Edinburgh, which was John Swinney's domain.

> "Maureen McKenna has been an effective Director of Education, much the best that Glasgow has had since it was set up as an independent authority in 1996," reckons Bloomer.

However, on the issue of the Newlands Junior College she seems to have had a blind-spot. It was not her idea and she was lukewarm about its development. Although she initially seconded Iain White to allow him to develop the concept further, she later became opposed to its development. Her viewpoint seems to have been that public sector secondary schools in Glasgow were highly capable of adapting to meet the needs of all young people and therefore did not require outside help. She was sceptical about private sector involvement in education and her first meeting with McColl did not get off to a good start. Perhaps McColl might have couched his request in more diplomatic terms. He described to McKenna that the junior college's intention was to "pick up young people who were dropping by the wayside but had potential."

"We're not looking for bampots," he is reported to have said.

This did not go down well with the director and her advisers. Indeed, the derogatory reference to "bampots" was raised in subsequent meetings. The term "bampots" has a particular resonance in Glasgow, meaning a troublemaker who was capable of doing stupid and dangerous things.

Yet bampot was exactly the term which signalled that Newlands Junior College was seeking to help those who had become disengaged with school yet showed potential to make it into a positive destination with appropriate help. The junior college was *not* looking for excessively disruptive or violent people who would have previously found themselves in specialist behavioural establishments.

Nonetheless, the all-important personal chemistry between the two got off to a bad start — and it never properly recovered.

Later, when the SNP won control of the council in Glasgow, McColl reached out to build a positive relationship with the leader Susan Aitken. Surely with Swinney and Aitken, both being Scottish National Party politicians, the Newlands project would be given a green light to continue? McColl recalls initial success with Councillor Aitken, who clearly understood the issues and expressed sympathy. However, the council leader and the chief executive Annemarie O'Donnell, who became a tacit supporter of the junior college and its innovation, had much more pressing issues averting the national industrial dispute by teachers and agreeing a pay deal, and resolving the long-running equal pay dispute for female council staff. All of this placed acute pressure on council funding that was already extremely tight.

Here, it can be argued, that McColl's team failed to understand the structures of local government in Scotland. While a council's chief executive might appear to be a superior of the director of education and social work, they would not be able to 'direct' a director of education on what to do about purely educational or social work policy. Education and social work are both statutory positions, and the directors are statutory advisers to the council on their areas of expertise. McKenna with her mammoth budget to pay for teachers, school buildings and educational support was in a dominant position and had considerable freedom of action.

"Maureen McKenna was not well disposed towards the Newlands initiative. In the circumstances, what happened was the best that we could have hoped for, in that she left it up to individual head teachers to decide whether they were prepared to recommend pupils from their schools or not," says Bloomer.

Others believed it was more nuanced than this and that McKenna could not tell head teachers *not* to support the junior college but it was up to them whether they 'could find any candidates that met the criteria.' The original intention was to take up to 60 pupils from secondary schools in the Southside of Glasgow, not the whole city. There are 11 secondary schools south of the River Clyde. Over the pilot, nine schools ended up sending pupils.

"In the approved area, the majority of the schools cooperated to some extent. But the fact that the head teachers all knew that the Director of Education was opposed to it, would not have helped," admits Bloomer.

Bloomer wrote the Skills System programme and became an adviser to the board of trustees.

"I was relatively closely involved up until the time of its closure," he says.

There now needed to be a decision about who would lead the new establishment. Gerrard and White had summed up the required qualities in a further report: *"The most important NJC teaching staff member to be recruited will be the Principal."* As this junior college was homing in on helping individual students find gainful employment, Skills Development Scotland was asked to assist in developing the Principal's job specification. It set out what it saw as the essential skills and attributes for this leader. The Principal had to be academically qualified in areas of education and business and have experience of working within the Scottish education system. The candidate required excellent leadership and communication skills and an ability to liaise with teachers, administrators and all staff involved in NJC operations. The candidate needed to be creative in the development of personal skills training within the college, and familiar with relevant HSE [Health, Safety and Environmental] legislation as it applies to school buildings and pupils.

Moreover, the Principal needed to be conversant with the Scottish Qualifications Authority's (SQA) procedures and requirements to become an SQA approved centre and have experience in course development and approval within the SQA's framework. The junior college was also aiming to deliver work-based qualifications rooted in the modern 21st century workplace.

With Iain White's personal imprint already on the junior college proposal, it appeared he was a shoe-in. But, like many a worthy plan, it took much longer than anticipated to secure the right man.

CHAPTER SEVEN:
White Heat:
The Forging of a Founding Figure

The educational figure who set the compass for the Newlands Junior College was something of a self-confessed maverick. But Iain White was exactly the right man in the right place for this job of Principal of Newlands Junior College. White was a vastly experienced head teacher in his late 50s who was shaped by his own West of Scotland upbringing. As a young adult, he knew his destiny was to become a teacher determined to make a difference to people's lives.

Iain White was born in Greenock in 1954, with his working-class parents raised in the industrial town on the River Clyde. Iain's father, Henry, known as 'Wee Harry' was born in 1917, while his mother, Margaret Cameron came from Argyllshire before settling in Greenock. Harry, the youngest of three brothers and a sister, had a hard upbringing and this made him fight to improve not only his status in life but the position of others less fortunate. Harry's Scottish socialist mindset and a determination to do better for himself and his family had a deep influence on his son.

During the dark days of the 1930s depression, when regular work across the west of Scotland was hard to find, Harry was encouraged to stick in at school and took his Highers.

> "He had aspirations to become a doctor and go to university. Looking back, it was a ridiculous aspiration because his uncle ensured he got work as an apprentice. He said he can remember being in tears when his mother told him he wasn't going to have any more education," says White. [32]

So Harry was destined not for the operating theatre of a hospital but the work bench as a joiner. Wee Harry, now 16, signed indentures and set out with the intention of 'being the best *jiner* he could possibly be' and to grab every opportunity for self-improvement, including night school in Paisley. In 1939, with war on the horizon, he was dispatched to the Orkney islands to build accommodation huts at Scapa Flow for the Royal Navy. He received his call-up and later became a Royal Navy diver. In 1940, Harry married Margaret

---

32 Interview with Iain White by the author, June 2019

Cameron, who had been working in service, and while he was away at sea she enlisted in the ATS, Auxiliary Territorial Service, although by then she had fallen pregnant. Harry returned to Greenock in 1946, attending Jordanhill College to train as a technical teacher. He taught at Port Glasgow High School and Mount Junior Secondary before landing a job as head of technical at St Mary's Junior Secondary in Greenock. In later years, Harry became head teacher at Castlehead High School in Paisley. Harry White had a rewarding career in teaching and was heavily involved with youth employment on the local area committee, which aimed to get young people out of school and into jobs.

Iain White was born at home in a post-war pre-fab in the Valley district of Greenock, moving as an infant with his family to a new council flat in the west end of the town. In Renfrewshire, in the 1950s and 1960s, church on Sunday with children attending Sunday school was still an expected weekend activity. Iain White says his parents were not overtly religious, and his father enjoyed a few drinks at the Masonic lodge and later Ardgowan Club bowling section, but the New Testament Bible teaching of Jesus's life and the poetry of Burns had a moral impact on a young man.

> "I often think of Oscar Wilde's description of a cynic as 'a man who knows the price of everything and the value of nothing', my father was the flip side of this. I think from an early age he inculcated a Presbyterian work ethic in us."

This encouraged Iain to try hard and stay on to undertake his exams at Greenock High School, becoming the first in his family to go to university. A neighbour began teaching the chanter to Iain, aged 12, and this sparked a lifelong passion for the Highland bagpipes. He joined the 1st Port Glasgow Boys' Brigade Pipe Band, which won the world juvenile pipe band championships and champion of champions for junior pipe bands in 1972. He progressed into adult piping competitions, winning more prizes, and played on the school cruises on the Clyde-built SS Nevasa and SS Uganda. Later, he joined the grade one Paisley Pipe Band, sponsored by Seagram's whisky company and known as The 100 Pipers, after their premium whisky brand, then piped with the British Caledonian Airways band, representing the Scottish airline at the Royal Albert Hall in London. But the commitment to both rehearsal and competition became too arduous for a student studying for his university finals.

Harry had started playing golf after the war and took his son for rounds on the municipal courses in Inverclyde. Golf, along with the pipes and Burns's poetry, became another of White's abiding pursuits. Robert Burns' universal message about the worth of all people struck a deep chord with White who would become a leading Burns speaker and a Senior Vice President of the Greenock Burns Club, the Mother Club and the oldest Burns club in the world. *"I've probably got a handful of heroes in my life, Burns is one of them,"* says White. His first public speaking engagement was giving the Toast to the Lassies at the Glasgow University Botanical Society's Burns Supper, where he was pleasantly surprised by the laughter his speech generated. Then, when the Royal West of Scotland Boat Club on the Esplanade in Greenock, asked him to speak, his journey as a Burns orator began. Years later, a pinnacle for White, decked in his mother's Cameron tartan, was delivering the Immortal Memory at the Royal & Ancient Golf Club at St Andrews.

This distinctive melting pot of Scottish influences helped forge a future teacher who was prepared to speak with an independent mind.

> "My family instilled in me a sense of standing by your principles. What was right and what was wrong. My dad used to say 'Iain, if something's not right, you've got to say it's not right'. When I was making my speech at the Govan High School centenary dinner in 2010 at the City Chambers in Glasgow, I said that advice had made me quite happy in the morning when I'm standing looking at myself in the mirror, shaving, but it's also got me into a lot of trouble over the years."

During his university summer vacation he worked in Scott's shipyard which gave him a respect for the skills of the local working people. There was a surge of pride in what he witnessed: *"I was in awe of the engineering skills displayed by many people in the yard."*

Iain White accepted a place to study Biological Sciences at the University of Glasgow but instead of a student flat off Byres Road, in Glasgow, he stayed at home. His ambition now was to become a teacher.

> "I don't know exactly why, but I think the fact that my father derived so much pleasure from his work as a teacher. He spent his life making a difference for young people who maybe weren't in the most advantaged situation."

Iain White earned a BSc honours degree, including passes in botany and plant physiology.

"It didn't really matter to me what I was doing because I was leaving university to become a teacher. However, I found the biological sciences absolutely fascinating."

Iain's father had predicted that biological sciences would be the future in schools. While chemistry, physics and mathematics were required for the next generation of engineers and scientists, there were not enough biology teachers. And if Iain White wanted to move up the career ladder and become a principal teacher, with an incremental rise in pay, then he should work as a biology teacher.

Iain White claims that psychometric testing shows he is an introvert. He says "*any extroversion in me is learned behaviour*". Yet he was able to overcome his natural introversion, helped by his Burns public orations. He learned to be more out-going in the classroom and his first teaching job was at Cowdenknowes High School in Greenock in 1977. He was the only biology teacher, straight out of Jordanhill Teacher Training College and armed with a Diploma in Education.

"The previous biology teacher had apparently lost the will. The classroom was a mess and the lab was in disarray. The school leaving age had recently been raised to 16 and there were now non-certificate science classes for those biding their time before getting out of school," says White. "I remember asking, 'What do I teach them?' and I was told, 'Anything you like'. I had to stand on my own two feet."

The Renfrewshire school system was divided into the junior and senior high schools. The Conservative-led local council had resisted the idea of going totally into the comprehensive state system and Cowdenknowes was a junior high, which only went to S4. It did not do much in terms of academic subjects, which were then Ordinary and Higher grade examinations. However, this was in flux when White arrived and the school was in its second year as a fully-fledged comprehensive. It had been an all-boys' school but S1 and S2 were now mixed, with S3 and S4 all boys.

"It was like two schools within the one school. For a teacher, the art of survival was important in the upper school because a lot of the boys didn't want to be there. They thought they were going to leave school and this wasn't happening. You could not turn your back to write on the blackboard. Hey, what a place to learn."

In those first crucial months at home, Harry would offer advice in his fireside chats as his son struggled to maintain a sense of what was happening.

> "He had worked in this school 30 years before in its previous iteration as a junior secondary. There were some teachers that he still knew. They looked after me and gave me essential tips."

These were the wise educational owls in the staff room who understood that an idealistic new recruit was finding it hard to get a handle on what coal-face secondary education was all about. The biology department had its sanctuary, a south-facing laboratory and greenhouse, which allowed White's cultivated plants to flourish, while his department kept living animals, including gerbils, rats, rabbits, and even budgies. Biology as a subject was in the ascendency. The discovery of DNA and RNA, the rise of sex education and the need for human biology, were making it a vital subject and teaching opportunities across Scotland increased to reflect this. The school advertised for a principal biology teacher and White landed the job. It was his first step up the career ladder. He was only 28.

> "These were the good days. I started to really love teaching. This was a school that was on the up and up. We had a head teacher called Graham Harcus who was very supportive."

Harcus, a young head teacher in his mid-30s, encouraged White to continue his educational training and undertake a Master of Education postgraduate qualification. He was given time off from the school's working timetable to attend college lectures. Later, Harcus went off to become a Deputy Director of Education at Strathclyde Region.

> "He was an inspiration. I used to watch folk whom I admired and see what they were doing well and try and emulate that. On the other hand, others I didn't admire as much, I tried to excise that from my being," he says. "My drive and aspirations for promotion was so I could get to a place where I could make a real difference."

From Greenock, White applied to Rothesay Academy and arrived there as Assistant Rector at the age of 33. He landed the job and his boss was Andy Gilmour, a 'most wonderful guy'. After the Argyll House interview in Dunoon, White was told by Gilmour:

> "I expect you to do this job very well. I won't be crawling all over you needing to know the minutiae about what you're doing. You just keep me up to date with what's happening and I'm sure that things will work out fine."

It was a lesson in the delegation of authority. There was also a move to give schools greater control of their own finances, and Rothesay was one of six on a pilot scheme.

> "Andy was a visionary and an innovator and he could see the opportunities of the head-teacher deciding on how to use the school's budget. It allowed a certain amount of flexibility that was more suited to local learning circumstances. This is something I've always believed is vital for head teachers to have."

White spent several years in Rothesay, then became Deputy Headmaster at Port Glasgow High, which meant less travelling. The pupil feedback from a group of second-year youngsters explained the White method. '*He's dead strict. He's a great laugh and he never, ever shouts at you,*' stated one pupil. "*For me, it was being strict for them, not for me, so they can do the best that they possibly can,*" says White.

Iain White was also learning about the preparation of young people for the trauma of the workplace. He understood they needed more support before heading out into the 'big, bad world'. This was the genesis of what would become the Future Skills System, which would connect young people with the idea of work and was later rolled out at Govan High School. White had been at Port Glasgow High for just over two years when his wife, Gail, spotted an advert in the *Glasgow Herald*'s recruitment pages. "*That would be a nice and handy job for you at Govan High School,*" she pointed out. He applied, got an interview at the education department's headquarters in 126 Bath Street. Later that day, Archie Morton, the divisional education officer, phoned Port Glasgow High and White took the call. "*Congratulations, Iain. You did well, you got the job.*" Wee Harry — who died a year later in 1995 as he approached 80 — was fiercely proud of his son.

CHAPTER EIGHT

Rough Stuff:
The Challenges of Govan High School

The place-name 'Govan' has intense social meaning in Glasgow. It was a tough, working-class district of tenement rows forged in the shadows of the clanking shipyard cranes. Decades of post-war blight had ravaged the district bringing high levels of urban deprivation, poverty and generational unemployment.

Iain White was 40 and in his prime when he arrived as head teacher at Govan High School in May 1994. As he steered his Ford Escort towards the school, turning off the motorway at the Hillington roundabout, then onto the Renfrew Road, onto Shieldhall Road, past the great whisky bottling plant, he thought; *Iain, you've done it this time! You're on your own.*

The maverick had finally arrived in a role where he could make a difference. He was on his own, with no senior figures to moderate his thinking, or tell him how *not* to run the show. On his first day, the deputy head Donald McPhail, a decent man in his late 50s, welcomed Iain and, before an expected introductory tour to meet the staff, invited him to take a drive in his car. They drove up into the Wine Alley and Teucharhill, where there were several burned-out vehicles. The walls were all daubed in graffiti, the smashed-up playparks were covered in broken glass, the alleyways strewn with rubbish and soiled mattresses and furniture, and there were homes with the windows boarded up with frames of steel. The population of Greater Govan had plummeted from 150,000 people in the Census of 1951 to fewer than 30,000 by 2001. The scale of the depopulation had led to a significant reduction in services creating a dislocated community where those with better prospects had moved out, leaving behind those with multiple social challenges and issues with anti-social behaviour.

The school's catchment area was one of the worst in terms of social deprivation in Britain. Over 60% of pupils were on free school meals, an indicator of the poverty level. Its boundaries were the Glasgow district border in the west, the M8 motorway in the south, the River Clyde, once the heart-beat of the Upper Clyde shipbuilding, in the north, and to the Copeland Road, home of the mighty Glasgow Rangers.

"This will set your eyes on the conditions of some of our young people coming out in the morning," said McPhail.

It certainly shocked White but his real lessons were back in the school. The school was a total and complete nightmare for pupils and for staff. Morale was rock bottom. The gang culture of territorial groups within the area often spilled out into scuffles and fights not just in classrooms but any area where pupils mixed. It was a powder keg, all day, every day.

> "The level of aggression and violence in the place was terrible. My immediate thought was 'What the hell are the adults up to around here?' if this is what the school is like. You can't blame the young people, you have to lay it at the door of the adults."

His Road to Damascus moment was in the English department corridor when there was a rammy of banging desks, shouting and serious disruption by a class of out of control 14-year-olds.

> "I was walking through the English department witnessing the noise and abuse and I thought: 'What the fuck are you doing here, Iain? Because it was a total nightmare."

He could just accept this was the state of things, throw in the towel, and get out, or he could stay and try and do something about it. He remembered his father's encouragement. *"If something isn't right, you've got to fix it, and stand up for it."* White had a hunch that the silent majority of pupils actually did not want the violence and disruption in their school but were unable to do much about it.

His solution to regain control was to put more rigour and discipline into the school. Central to this was zero-tolerance of physical violence, long before the term zero-tolerance policy was imported from New York and came into common parlance. This became a principle rule for Govan High School.

> "Basically, if you hit anybody, you were in big trouble. I made it clear to young people that if you hit anyone – it doesn't matter who they are – you are in the wrong."

He rationalised this by saying that if someone hit you and you hit them back, then you are culpable too in the creation of a fight. Within days, a number of consistently violent pupils including young women were being marched out of the school and told to go home. Over the next month, a stream of rule-breakers were being turfed out for physical violence in classrooms, corridors, dinner hall, toilets and playground. Inevitably, it led to a flow of irate parents chapping on the head teacher's door to complain. Iain White quickly needed a tactical response to handle these fraught encounters. He learned not to invite parents into his office for a private one-to-one meeting, but in another more public room, preferably with another colleague in attendance.

One angry parent explained to the new head teacher why his son smashed another in the face with his fist.

"That's the way we do it around here," said the parent menacingly.

"Actually, I don't care too much what you do down your *bit*, but last time I checked this is ma *bit* and I decide what happens in here. What I'm telling you is we're no having people hitting one another," replied White.

The parent, jarred by White's push-back, leaning over the table and raised his voice. Increasingly, hot and bothered, he started banging the table with his fist and swearing.

"Look, Mr Smith, there's only one person getting excited here, and it's no me," warned the head teacher.

White stated calmly that the meeting was over and he asked the parent to leave but the stream of invective was louder, and much more personal.

"We're now entering the realms of breach of the peace and threatening behaviour, and I have a witness here. So you have a choice, either you go right now or I'm gonna lift the phone and you'll get lifted."

The exclusion procedures are governed by the Schools General (Scotland) Regulations of 1975 and were amended by the Education Scotland Act 1980. Under the regulations, an education authority shall not refuse a pupil, who is ordinarily resident in their area, admission to a school under their management or exclude a pupil from such a school unless the parent or the pupil refuse to comply with rules and regulations required to maintain discipline.

Several more weeks passed and another irate parent was up to the school about his son being sent home. White walked into a room where the parent was already sitting next to the excluded boy.

"Before you say a word Mr White, you are 100% correct. A fuckin' telt him, a fuckin' telt him, ya shouldnae have hit him in the school, you should have fuckin' waited and got him doun the road," said the parent.

White knew then that his zero-tolerance message was out in Govan, that things had changed. While it was unfortunate that the violence might well have been displaced beyond the school back into the community, at least the high school was showing a zero-tolerance to violence and this allowed the school to reclaim its position as a place of learning.

In an effort to sort out the territorial gang violence in the school, White enlisted the help of the local police superintendent who ran G Division. This made a big difference to behaviour in classes.

Senior pupil representatives from all of Glasgow's schools were invited to the City Chambers in George Square to discuss aspects of school life. They were asked about the negative affect territorialism and gang-related activities spilling into schools was having on learning and social interaction. Many school reps were recounting stories of aggression, violence and police involvement. The room fell silent when a young female voice called out: "*That sort of thing doesnae happen at Govan High!*" When the presenter homed in on the pupil and asked, "*How come?*" She replied: "*Because Mr White widnae have it!*"

It took time, but White and his teaching staff began transforming the culture at Govan High School, making it an exemplar in Glasgow for helping young people. It went through several cycles, each one raising the level of discipline and relative attainment.

> "The young people were good. It was just a very small number that had to be dealt with so that everybody else could get on with stuff. We managed that."

Another pupil on the periphery of acceptable behaviour found that working with plants was a way to calm his aggression and he ended up as a gardener with Glasgow City Council, successfully grappling with the Latin names for various species. White had learned from his mentor Andy Gilmour about the power of delegation. He developed the knack of getting people to do things. White reckons this is about leadership.

> "My leadership style is facilitate and enable, rather than command and control. It is about getting folk involved in decision-making, and the direction the school is going in and indeed being leaders," he says.

It reached its height as an essential part of his modus operandi at Newlands.

CHAPTER NINE:
A Driving Force:
Business Steps Up to the Mark

Everyone nodded heartily in agreement that Newlands Junior College was, indeed, a brilliant idea. Time and again, McColl won over converts in the private meetings and dinners he hosted across central Scotland. A cross-section of business figures from various industry sectors shared his concern, lamenting the failure of a system which let down too many young Scottish people. More must be done to encourage disengaged young people and prevent them falling behind and stepping away from the jobs market. He penned a raft of personal letters explaining the rationale, seeking substantial financial commitment from wealthy donors to get this underway.

In January 2013, McColl wrote to Sir Ian Wood, the Aberdeen businessman who had built up the Wood Group to become one of Scotland's leading engineering companies. Sir Ian was a former chair of Scottish Enterprise and had been deeply involved in the skills agenda for Scotland. He had made strong recommendations on vocational training and employment in his *Commission for Developing Scotland's Young Workforce*, which he chaired.[33] He identified "the importance of business and industry working with schools and colleges as a key factor in ensuring young people are more prepared for employment."

Sir Ian's findings showed that employers had "lost the habit of employing young people", and only 29% of employers recruited young people and only 13% of employers took on an apprentice. One of his loudest calls was for the roll-out of Modern Apprenticeships in industries where young people might have the chance of building long-term careers. He called for an additional 5,000 Modern Apprenticeships by 2020.

Sir Ian's executive team at the John Wood Group [now Wood plc] included Bob Keiller, who also became a chairman of Scottish Enterprise. Sir Ian wrote back to McColl.

> "I have sent the key parts of your Newlands Junior College proposal and file note to Bob Keiller and to Allister Langlands at Wood Group

33 Commission for Developing Scotland's Young Workforce, chaired by Sir Ian Wood, June 2014.

and Bob has indicated he would be happy to chat to you. I think his initial reaction was the same as mine, that the concept is absolutely right but the cost will be high both capital and revenue wise and this kind of development is what should take place within the main school system."

While Sir Ian wished him good luck, this was a clear indication that well-connected business associates were reticent about stepping into the area of secondary education in Scotland.

"Jim was probably disappointed about the level of support from big business. I assume that he thought there would be enough supporters so that Newlands could run on the basis of contributions of £100,000 each for five years," says Keir Bloomer.

Many business people, while expressing deep reservations about the ability of Scotland's educators to provide the necessary calibre of candidate for the future workplace, did not feel that they should interfere in secondary school education unless they were invited to do so. There was one notable exception: Sir Arnold Clark, one of Scotland's most exceptional entrepreneurs.

"The relationship with Arnold Clark began with Alex Stewart," recalls Eddie Hawthorne, the chief executive and group managing director of Arnold Clark. "He came to see me and he painted a picture of Jim's vision. He asked if we would become involved. It was very timely because I was doing a quarterly review with Sir Arnold. I mentioned to Sir Arnold and Lady Clark that this was something that Jim was looking to get off the ground. I thought we should become involved, and Sir Arnold agreed." [34]

There is no doubt this was a massive boost for the fledgling junior college, and Arnold Clark would become one of its stalwart supporters. The Hillington-based private family business, with a turnover of £4.2 billion in 2019, and valued at £1 billion, and profits of £113 million, represents 27 different motor manufacturing companies in the UK including top of the range Mercedes-Benz, BMW, Alfa Romeo, through to mid-range Citroen, Vauxhall, SEAT, and Ford, and now electric cars from car-makers. In 2019, the firm sold 305,616 cars with 30% new and 70% used vehicles.

But, most importantly, Arnold Clark is a people business, employing 13,000 people with Eddie Hawthorne wanting this to increase to 15,000 over the

---

34 Interview with the author, January 2020.

next few years. There were over 5,000 people in the Glasgow area alone plus another 4,000 across the rest of Scotland, and the average age was under 34. The old-fashioned male-dominated motor trade was going through a transformation and it had a high demand for apprentices keen to pursue a career working with cars and vans.

> "We have always been very big into apprenticeships as a company. We currently have over 900 apprentices on our books. Sir Arnold always started off in the training school and he really liked the training aspect of our business. But what he really liked was the ability to give people who had a talent an opportunity. This is what he liked about Jim McColl's model," says Hawthorne.

The Arnold Clark boss understood that the junior college's model was addressing the issue of young Scots who were not achieving their potential in mainstream education.

> "We understood it was a pilot education programme to see whether taking a slightly different approach to education and training would work. And I believe it has," he says.

Sir Arnold Clark, who remained chairman until his death in April 2017, wanted to go ahead with supporting the Newlands Junior College, and Hawthorne was invited to become one of the first trustees. He remained a trustee until the eventual closure.

Since 2008, Arnold Clark had been collaborating with the Prince's Trust Scotland in its 'Get Into Cars' scheme, a six-week intensive programme where young people had an alternative route to finding a Modern Apprenticeship by gaining hands-on experience working in an Arnold Clark showroom or vehicle workshop. If the trainees, aged from 16 to 25 years old, completed the programme successfully, they gained the opportunity of becoming full-time apprentices.

> "What we saw through our Get Into Cars programme was they were slightly older young people than Jim McColl's target group, and it was working well. If you gave these young people an opportunity to progress in education and training, they became really fulfilled employees, who were hard-working and loyal to the business," he says.

With Newlands, Sir Arnold understood all they were doing was shifting the age-group down a little bit to help those who were skipping school but had potential.

"Once Sir Arnold and Lady Clark agreed to support the venture, it was left to me to get on with it. Again, it started to work," says Hawthorne.

As a company, Arnold Clark already had a substantial commitment to training its people. A training college for mechanics and motor engineers was set up in Glasgow in the early 1970s by ten motor dealers with Arnold Clark as a founding member. The college was created to unlock the funding from the RTITB [Road Transport Industry Training Board] which was set up to improve workplace safety standards. In 2003, Arnold Clark bought all the remaining shares of the other dealers and took over the Glasgow college. It was rehoused in South Street and became GTG Training, followed by a GTG Training college in Wolverhampton, with a focus on automotive technical and transport training with an IT and business skills division running approved courses. GTG Training, regulated by Ofsted, the UK's Office for Standards in Education and Skills, would become a pathway for many of the Newlands Junior College cohort who wanted to develop motor industry careers. The first graduate was Giancarlo Pelosi, who became a time-served mechanic. What Arnold Clark was already doing, chimed with one of Sir Ian Wood's recommendations: "*that Modern Apprenticeships should be aligned with the skills required to support economic growth.*" While Arnold Clark and indeed ScottishPower, another significant employer in Glasgow, could see the merits in assisting Newlands, it was a difficult prospect to sell as another of the trustees, Scott Black, found out.

......

Scott Black is a former pupil of Govan High School. He attended the secondary from 1975 until 1981. Black is one of Scotland's most respected headhunters and managing director of the Edinburgh-based executive recruitment firm FWB Park Brown, formerly Finlayson, Wagner and Black, which he co-founded more than 25 years ago. He has a background in accountancy but moved into the recruitment game and has an easy-going and analytical nature which allows him to get along with all kinds of people. He has been responsible for finding and putting top executives into leading companies and, for four years until July 2019, he was president of Edinburgh Chamber of Commerce.

He has a family and is a fitness fanatic who has run several marathons, and enjoys long-distance hiking and cycling and, by many measures, he can be judged as one of Scotland's most influential business figures. Shortly before Newlands Junior College opened both Black and McColl were in Houston on business (FWB Park Brown have offices in Texas to service the international

64

energy industry) and they met in a city hotel one evening for a meal.

> "I was bending Jim's ear over a variety of matters, and we seemed to spend an increasing amount of time over the following year talking about education in Scotland," says Black. [35]

Black recalled growing up in the area and classes at Govan at the end of the 1970s. A previous generation had all left school and headed off to apprenticeships in the local shipyards, but when Black was contemplating leaving, the Upper Clyde yards were disappearing and there were not enough engineering jobs.

> "I certainly wasn't the brightest person in that year at secondary school. Probably middle of the pack. But only three or four went on to university, including me. There was a whole bunch of guys who were brighter than me, and although I don't know where all of them ended up, at the time they weren't achieving their potential," he says.

McColl was curious and asked Black why this should be. He explained pupils were not engaged by the school, which just felt like a place you went. *"It was a bit of a hardship and the teachers wanted you to tow the line. If you didn't do that, you could quickly be sidelined and fall out of school,"* he said.

Black attended Drumoyne Primary School at Cardonald, before going to the 'big school'. He lived in Shieldhall and believes he was kept going purely because his parents — his dad worked in the health service —were keen on him attending school. Black went to the University of Paisley, which became the University of the West of Scotland, and then undertook a postgraduate diploma in finance at the University of Strathclyde.

> "I was on that cusp though. Govan was hammered by unemployment and over 50% of people were out of work. I said to Jim the kids were not all bad kids. They hadn't turned up at school disengaged at the start, this just happened. They didn't want to run about breaking into shops and spraying buildings with paint, or cause mayhem, they were just kids. And because they didn't engage in school for whatever reason, then all these other things happened. But they were bright."

Scott Black had returned to Govan High as a school visitor, meeting with Iain White whom he respected. McColl listened with growing interest and gradually shared his ideas for the new junior college with Black. He finished off by asking if Black would join the board of trustees. It seemed like a neat

---

35 Interview with Scott Black by the author, September 2019.

and fitting idea, and the influential Glasgow-born headhunter agreed.

.....

One of Black's strengths as a trustee was his network of contacts. Armed with his address book, he was pulled in to help with fund-raising. It cost around £1.2 million a year to run Newlands Junior College, although expenditure was £797,000 in the 2014-2015, when income was £1.23 million. Over the next four years expenditure was £1.24 million in 2016, £1.15 million in 2017, £2.26 million in 2018, which included the settlement of the building refurbishment costs, and £843,616 in the final year.

Year End	Income	Expenditure
30 June 2015	£1,229,529	£796,896
30 June 2016	£837,228	£1,245,511
30 June 2017	£1,026,225	£1,152,496
30 June 2018	£1,533,774	£2,259,543
30 June 2019	£1,260,052	£843,616
Total	**£5,886,808**	**£6,298,062***

* The difference between Income and Expenditure was squared by payments from Clyde Blowers Capital and Arnold Clark.

Income, made up from one-off or recurring charitable contributions, fluctuated over the duration but in total was £5,886,808. The college needed a steadier and regular commitment of ten subscribers prepared to put in at least £100,000 per year, or £500,000 over the five years of the project. In his initial calculations, McColl anticipated that the Scottish Government and Glasgow Council would become two of the anchor subscribers, and he would require another eight from business people, wealthy individuals or their organisations.

From September 2014 until 30th June 2015, the college received £904,000 in donations, and £320,990 of grants from the Scottish Government and Glasgow Council. In total, the Scottish Government provided £500,000 as a capital contribution, then further grants of £708,000.

In 2016, the college brought in £837,228 towards its costs, although this improved to £1.03 million in 2017, £1.53 million in 2018, and £1.26 million in the final year. McColl's own company Clyde Blowers Capital was one of the ten, joined by Arnold Clark who were committed supporters from the start, along with the likes of Weir Group, the pumps and engineering group, Malcolm Group, the logistics and distribution company, with its headquarters at Linwood.

Black tried to entice more businesses to support the college.

> "I ultimately proved to be unsuccessful on that score. We could get people to talk to us, and get them to come to the college and see what was going on. We had several evenings and had a highly successful Night at the College and it worked really well and a few people gave us money," he says.

But not nearly enough. Wealthy individuals are asked to fund a great number of charitable causes. Education is one of these matters which people understand is hugely important, but people see it as the state's role to fund this kind of special education. While the well-heeled might send their children to an independent school in Edinburgh or Glasgow, this was something entirely different.

There can be no doubt about McColl and Stewart's personal commitment. Certainly, they were wealthy Scots, but they regularly bridged funding shortfalls and payment delays from their own pockets. In the final two years, Clyde Blowers Limited put in £750,000 to the college, Clyde Blowers Capital, one of McColl's private equity funds, donated £200,000 over the period, while two other McColl businesses, David Brown Group, based in Huddersfield, and Hydreco, donated a total of £45,000. In return for services undertaken by Clyde Blowers Limited, in East Kilbride, the charity paid fees of £68,000. Arnold Clark donated £290,930 over the final two years, with Eddie Hawthorne personally stepping in to ensure there was working capital for the college. In addition, Newlands received a further £30,000 government grant.

.....

Alex Stewart preferred to calculate the college's finances in a different way: this was the entitlement of individual young people to their fair share of tax-funded resources. Every child in Scotland has a monetary value attached to their life by the state. According to Audit Scotland, the national average spend per primary school pupil in 2018/2019 was £5,259, while the national average per secondary school pupil was £7,157. There are council variations, with primary pupils in Shetland averaging £8,041 and in the Western Isles £9,153, while those in Falkirk average £4,655 with Argyll & Bute £6,490. We must be cautious about comparisons because Scottish councils with higher per head spending do not always have a higher proportion of pupils attaining higher levels of numeracy and literacy. There are many factors at play including teacher demographics, local choices on staffing, and contract costs for building and upkeep of school estate. When it comes to secondary education, the magic number in Glasgow is £7,600. That is what each school is given for each pupil per annum and is an average figure.

> "At the outset this was not the case, at the beginning what we thought we could achieve was on an individual rather than a whole total. As soon as you mention the figure of £1 million, people will say it is too expensive. On average, in Glasgow, it is £7,600 per student at the start of their secondary education and this goes up over five years to educate every student," Stewart explains.

Here is the rub: pupils who leave at 16 only get four years of secondary education, which was substantially less than those finishing after sixth year.

> "The children that come from families who are supportive and encouraging of the young person to remain in education until fifth and sixth year are getting more from the system. They get an extra two years of secondary schooling," he continues.

A cogent argument from the Newlands Junior College trustees was this extra two years came at the expense of those leaving education at 16. Hardly fair, they pointed out. If an individual child, born in a postcode of multiple deprivation rather than a leafy middle-class suburb, could be reclassified as a 'budget holder', should they not be entitled to the same amount of investment? Instead, under the present system, the young person is losing out by around £15,200.

Local government planners and statisticians are able to look at the birth rate in each city postcode and calculate whether a child is likely to remain in secondary education or move into the NEET category. From the trustees' point of view, each child should be entitled to the same amount.

> "Instead of the system in Glasgow treating everyone equally, it is fundamentally flawed. If we could view young people as individual 'budget holders', then they should be entitled to their money to be spent on giving them the best start to their lives," says Stewart.

Newlands Junior College's expectation was that the council would transfer the £15,200 to Newlands for the benefit of the students, with £1,200 coming from the Pupil Equity Fund given by the Scottish Government to schools in deprived postcodes and based on national eligibility criteria. This fund, part of the £750 million Attainment Scotland Fund, was assigned to the head teacher of the mainstream school which was previously attended by a Newlands student, and was never transferred to the student in whose name it was granted.

> "We could never even get that Pupil Equity Fund money for Newlands," he explains. "It would have made huge difference to us. It was supposed to follow the child."

Stewart later found out that the Pupil Equity Fund, set up in 2018 until the end of the sitting of Scottish Parliament, was massively under-spent across Scotland, particularly in Glasgow. This represented millions of pounds sitting in education budgets which could have been diverted to support students at Newlands.

While Stewart's financial logic appeared sound and equitable, it hit the buffers when it reached the *realpolitik* of education departments. His financial argument about holistic funding for young people has never been properly acknowledged and remains an unresolved issue for Scotland's politicians to grapple with.

Discussion on funding was an early roadblock. In January 2012, Elizabeth Buie, writing in the *TES Scotland* (TESS), reported:

> "One of Scotland's richest businessmen hopes to open Scotland's first junior vocational college for disaffected teenagers by August this year, but the funding package is still not in place. Jim McColl's dream of turning his former Clyde Union factory into the bespoke Newlands Junior College in Glasgow's Cathcart area is estimated to cost around £1 million per annum for the first two years, half for refurbishment and half for educational services." [36]

Glasgow City Council told McColl it could find no more than £100,000 from its education and development and regeneration budgets for each of the first two years. According to the article, Maureen McKenna wrote to McColl, stating:

> "The cost per pupil of the proposal is around £13,500, not including the building costs. This compares with around £5,500 for a secondary pupil, including building costs. This cost would be over and above what we are paying already for secondary education as there is no

---

36 Times Educational Supplement Scotland, January 2012.

saving generated by taking a small number of pupils out from different secondary schools. I am not in a position to be able to commit to that level of funding for an initiative."[37]

Instead, McKenna proposed a more cost-effective scholarship model which would leave selected S4 to S6 students in school but undertaking a reduced number of subjects with one day a week's work experience with a sponsoring business partner. McColl railed against McKenna's scholarship model declaring it a 'non-starter'.

> "You would not get me or another private-sector business seriously doing that. It is just another initiative set up to fail. You need to get these kids into a different environment and inspire them and motivate them on a daily basis," he told the TESS.

The TESS article continued: "Under his plan, 30 S3 pupils would be selected from ten secondaries in the southside of Glasgow to attend the college. They would follow a two-year programme with three strands: academic, vocational and life-skills. Originally intended to open last year, it should be up and running by Christmas at the latest."

But the project was already behind schedule, although architects were being commissioned to draw up plans to transform the derelict Minto Building premises at 6 Inverlair Avenue.

> "Mr McColl estimates that it will cost £500,000 to refurbish one floor of the building for the first cohort of pupils and a further £500,000 for the second year's group. These costs would be met by himself and supporters from the private sector. The education side of the project, however, — costing a projected £500,000 for each of the first two years — would, he hoped, be split three ways between the private sector, Glasgow City Council and the Scottish Government. The average cost per secondary pupil in Glasgow is £7,000 per year."

Glasgow City Council eventually agreed to pay £100,000 a year to support Newlands, while the Scottish Government contributed £500,000 towards the start-up costs, and later contributed a further £700,000.

The vocational providers were: City of Glasgow College; GTG Training (Arnold Clark); and Riverside Studios (for a limited period). The junior college was supported by a number of businesses, in the form of financial

---

37 TESS, Ibid.

contributions, provision of work experience, mentoring, offers of apprenticeships and jobs. Consequently, private funding from business and individuals made up the majority of junior college's funding.

CHAPTER TEN:
Cathcart Creation:
A Derelict Shell Becomes Place of Learning

The Minto Building in Inverlair Avenue in Cathcart was a derelict, four-storey shell in a parlous state and unfit for any kind of educational purpose. It was located in the south side of Glasgow, a street away from the White Cart Water which wends its way through the southern districts of the city, and it belonged to an international engineering company.

For many years it had been the training centre for the Weir Group and McColl had vivid memories of the place, spent at the workbenches and in the training rooms as an engineering apprentice at Weir's. The building, which now belonged to SPX Flow Group as leaseholders, would require significant investment in refurbishment, yet it had immense potential.

The trustees sought guidance on what needed to be done and Kier Construction, a design and construction firm, was invited to help with proposals to convert the ground floor of the existing building. In February 2012 a team of five design and planning managers from Kier Construction and a director of planning consultants M&E Consultants went on an initial inspection to assess the condition of the building's fabric. Could it be suitable for a junior college — and how much would it take to make it fit for purpose?

> "The building itself is classified as light industrial and is a steel framework with brickwork and cladding to the external walls, concrete floors. It was built in 1975 and is currently lying empty with evidence of severe water penetration in the main stair area which extends from the top down to the ground floor," said the report alarmingly.

The picture was not good. Green algae and water made the stairs unsafe and there was mould growing and water-sodden plaster throughout the building. The existing roof of wired glass extending over the length of the building had been covered with bitumen-impregnated fibreglass and a reflective coating. It was in a poor condition with a number of holes where rainwater poured in. The gutters were blocked and downpipes had disappeared allowing the water to spill out over the side of the building.

Yet the report said the external brickwork appeared sound and the modern

PVC double-glazed windows on the front were in a workable state, although all the mechanical and electrical cables were long passed their lifespan.

A structural engineer was recommended to carry out a full survey, with a detailed report to be undertaken on the roof to bring it up to standard for another 25 years.

> "The building and fabric should be brought up to current standards to thermal and sustainable levels sufficient to obtain a building warrant."

To turn this derelict place into a college, the entire internal partitions, flooring, suspended ceilings and redundant timbers were stripped out in a single operation to minimise the costs and limit future disruption. This would include remedial work to the stairs, allowing them to dry out over time. This would also mean the replacement of the existing ventilation with a new boiler system and ducting to heat the building. Along with a new water plant to service the canteen and toilet areas with an environmentally friendly system, there was a need for new efficient lighting, including emergency lighting and break glass points, to be designed and provided on the ground floor and compliant with building regulations.

This was not an inexpensive refurbishment. By July 2015, the cost of 'leasehold' improvements was £1.86 million, with computer equipment for the college of around £100,000.

Haa design, set up by Hugh Anderson in 1994, won the interior design and fit-out contract to make the refurbished space as engaging and interesting as its limitation would allow. The Glasgow-based consultancy had undertaken design work for Heriot-Watt University, University of the West of Scotland's new Lanarkshire campus, and Ayrshire College, and grabbed the opportunity.

> "Small in size, but grand in vision, the client required a mix of learning environments, from more traditional classrooms to informal break out zones. These spaces are all furnished to a high quality, with students encouraged to participate in academic learning as well as vocational training. Flexibility in the design and use of shared spaces was a key requirement for NJC, as student numbers are set to increase in coming years," said a case study by haa design, incorporated into SPACE Consultancy and Design, which was rebranded in 2018. [38]

It was designed as a space for 21st century learning in what was Activity-Led

---

38 SPACE Consultancy and Design, 2020. http://www.spacesolutions.co.uk/case-studies_ss/new-lands-junior-college

Design, understanding that learning takes place in a variety of contexts and each student learns in a different way. The formal classroom was only one setting but there was flexibility to expand classrooms equipping them with easily-movable furniture and science and lab benches.

The building still maintained its industrial feel, with exposed steel beams, and air-conditioning and ventilation ducts and pipework, but the smaller rooms and off-corridor booths were intimate and modern. The large circular Polo-mint ring lighting threw bright light into the canteen gathering area and new larger windows made the college feel airy and vibrant. In the foyer, a three-metre high, floor-to-ceiling letter 'N' was painted with the word NEWLANDS, while other key signage was loud and clear, and the canteen wall was stencilled with a set of black gear cogs representing the interconnection between engineering and science and the 'cogs' of learning.

On Wednesday, 28th September 2011, Iain White and Bill Gerrard met with Hugh Anderson in Cathcart where they spent two hours discussing the look, feel and the ambience. After the meeting, they visited the Minto Building. White wrote in his diary "*It has fantastic potential ... After lunch we visited Albert Park, the Weir's recreation ground just along the road. The grounds there afford great possibilities for environmental and sports/fitness activities.*"

Dr Gerrard said in his original report that the design of the room was about connecting both visually and physically the various group and individual learning spaces, so that "*learning can spill outside of the classroom and connect with other activities taking place within the school, and overlap with other teachers and administrative staff.*" This flexibility and informality was something the students would come to cherish and enjoy. This became part of the junior college's DNA.

The aim was to open the new junior college for session 2013/2014 but the building work took more time and Keir Bloomer became concerned:

> "It is now clear that Newlands Junior College will not be open in time for the start of the new session in August. The necessary modifications to the building cannot be completed within the few weeks that remain," he warned in March 2013. [39]

There were other matters to consider, including the recruitment of staff and young people and negotiations with Glasgow City Council were still going on.

---

39 Note to trustees: Newlands Junior College: Issues Influencing Possible Opening Dates, Keir Bloomer, 8 March 2013.

"The next occasion when a fresh S3 cohort of pupils could be recruited is August 2014. A start at that date would allow the programme to be implemented in the way that had always been intended. There would be no requirements to modify admission, curriculum or staffing arrangements," noted Bloomer.

The building was being decorated in an interesting way with the library – or the information centre – overlapping with the canteen, where integrated learning could be encouraged at break times when people were socialising and eating together. The furniture was selected by Steelcase, a global company with a strong reputation for designing products that helped foster flexible learning. This included the Node campus chair — dubbed the Dalek chairs by Newlands students — which included a desk, and an under-seat shelf for bags, and a set of wheels for rolling into different positions.

There was no escaping this was an industrial building attached to a major engineering factory with no traditional school playground, although students had access to the nearby Albert Park playing fields where they could undertake sports and other outdoor activities.

Underpinning all of this was the need to have excellent ICT facilities with desk-tops, servers, and modern digital kit. The Apple Mac was the computer of choice and no expense was spared in ensuring the latest educational packages were uploaded. Indeed, the junior college was well ahead of the rest of the city's state schools in its provision of laptops for learning. The irony for an education department so opposed to private sector involvement was Glasgow Council's agreement to continue to outsource the city's ICT department and service to schools through a £211 million contract with Canadian technology giant CGI, rolling out iPads to all senior pupils from October 2018. [40] By the start of 2020, 13,000 iPads had been given out to pupils and 3,000 to teachers, which were integrated through Apple's Classroom Manager software intended for 'educational transformation'.

The Minto Building proved that even an unlikely location could, with proper investment and thoughtful spatial design for learning, become a safe space where young people felt warmly connected.

"In many respects it worked in spite of itself. It was an old industrial building with no windows on one side. It did not really lend itself to being a school, stuck away in an area of housing and a community

---

40 CGI press release, 14 December 2017. www.cgi.com/uk/en-gb/news/glasgow-city-council-awards-seven-year-transformational-ict-outsourcing-contract-to-cgi

where none of the young people actually came from," says Scott Black.

At first impression, it didn't look like a most obvious 'positive destination'. But it was the teaching and support staff in the office, those in the canteen and driving the minibuses, all working in harmony, who really made it gel.

CHAPTER ELEVEN:
The Right Staff:
The Principal Appointments

Iain White and Gail, his wife, were celebrating his 60th birthday on a trip to Vienna over the Easter weekend in April 2014. On Good Friday, the 18th April, as the couple wandered around the Albertina art galleries, White's mobile phone pinged with an email from Angela Meikle, Jim McColl's personal assistant. It contained a long anticipated offer from the Scottish entrepreneur.

There had been a year-long delay caused by the extensive building work and the issue of securing the philanthropic funding. Keir Bloomer had suggested that the school might have opened in January 2014, but the trustees felt it was better to get everything properly in place and stay in sync with normal school dates. So White had been patiently getting on with his life. Now McColl was making a formal proposal.

> "Come and be the Principal at the college. You've already put your mark on the college with your thinking, why not come and really make it happen? We can work together on driving this change," encouraged McColl.

While it was a tantalising offer, White took the rest of his birthday weekend to mull it over with Gail before heading up to East Kilbride on Tuesday, 22nd April. After a cordial discussion with McColl, he accept the position. As a head teacher with many years under his belt, his salary would be around £80,000 a year. He handed in his notice, cleared his desk, said his goodbye to Govan and started in mid-May, joining Bloomer. There was no finished premises, no staff, no college and no young people.

> "At this stage, it was the easiest job that I'd ever had in education. It was a wonderful position to be in because we went from developing the concept to welcoming the first cohort into the college," says White.

The Principal would be responsible for the college's operational management, answerable to the board of trustees who would agree the strategic framework and purpose.

With building work well underway, the task of Bloomer and White was to find and employ the right kind of teaching staff. The college's requirements were relatively modest: an English teacher, a Maths teacher, an IT teacher, and a Science teacher, with one of this group being the Depute Principal supporting White, and acting as the Child Protection Officer.

> "We had a long discussion about how we should approach the recruitment. Jim McColl was keen to have this partnership with Glasgow City Council and its Education Services department to ensure the authorities were comfortable with the process, so the decision was made that we would go through the regular recruitment process," says White.

Bloomer and White wrote job specifications and the jobs were advertised in the usual channels for teaching opportunities in Scotland, including the *Times Educational Supplement Scotland* (TESS). The new college was deluged with interested applicants. The sifting process took time with interviews arranged and appointments made. For White it was about finding the right blend of experience, enthusiasm and flexibility to deal with what was an unknown project. His chosen deputy would become part of an incredible educational double-act

.....

Iain White had started the turn-around at Govan High School but it was the arrival of a new deputy head who managed to take it to another more positive level. While White was the 'philosopher king' and a figure of authority, the day-to-day operational affairs required a different kind of motivated individual. This was Philip Graham who arrived in May 2001 to become Principal Teacher of Behavioural Support at Govan High School. If White was later to be the heart of Newlands Junior College, Graham was the head and the brain, indeed the operating system of the college. Much of the influential tone of the junior college stemmed from Graham's calm and friendly demeanour.

Philip Graham is 15 years younger than Iain White. He was brought up in the middle-class, south-side of Glasgow in Newlands and attended Holyrood Secondary. When the teachers' strikes hit the state sector in Scotland, his aspirational parents moved him to St Aloysius' College in Garnethill, an academic, independent fee-paying Roman Catholic school. He went off to University of Glasgow to study accountancy.

> "I struggled through that and hated every single second of it but graduated in 1988 through gritted teeth," says Graham. [41]

---

41 Interview with Philip Graham by the author, June 2019.

78

He secured an apprenticeship as a chartered accountant with Stoy Hayward but lasted only two weeks. He approached the senior partner and admitted there had been a terrible mistake. Graham decided he really wanted to be a teacher. He was released from his obligations, learned to touch type before enrolling at the St Andrew's teacher training college in Milngavie. He studied to become a business studies and economics teacher, with the typing helping him teach administration courses as well.

As a newly-qualified teacher, he undertook supply teaching jobs awaiting a full-time appointment. In October 1993, he received a call from his sister-in-law, who knew a St Andrew's lecturer. A colleague's wife worked in Ladywell School in Dennistoun, in the East End of Glasgow. They wanted some relief cover and Philip was asked if he would like to take it on. The school building, the former Alexander's School, at 94 Duke Street, was a handsome sandstone building with a bell-tower, and five busts of the giants of the arts and literature, including Homer, Aristotle, Shakespeare, Michelangelo and Milton, yet it was a tough place for children with emotional and behavioural difficulties.

> "This was a complete eye-opener to me. This was something I had never seen in my life. These were children I had never seen the like of before. They were angry, aggressive, constantly swearing right in the teachers' faces. On day one, I couldn't believe what I was seeing. I couldn't believe the abuse the teachers were taking and they were letting it all wash over them while still managing to engage the children."

This baptism for Graham, earning £11,997 a year, was soon all about survival as a novice in the classroom jungle.

> "It was blatantly obvious that this place was all about relationships. The children were clinging to this place because it offered structure, trust and warmth. It offered open arms to children who were very, very fractured people," he says.

The head teacher was Anne Bombelli, an incredibly committed teacher who taught Philip Graham a great deal about such relationships. She had a long career in social, emotional and behavioural education at Ladywell. The school roll was only 30, with five classes, and a range of young people, from 12 to 16, who were withdrawn, violent, bullied and bullying. The class size was no more than six pupils. Many were from families where parents were out of their heads on drug addiction, and some were vulnerable to sexual abuse.

They were all-day pupils in full-time education who attended for the school week, rather than bussed in part-time from other state schools in the city.

What was a young teacher such as Philip Graham expected to impart to such a group of young people?

> "Academic outcomes were different from engagement in education. We had to engage them by using a subject, project or a theme. So we had a maths teacher who could calm her class by giving them reams and reams of mental arithmetic, which wasn't progressing them. It wasn't pedagogically sound but it meant for 35 minutes they had calm, and they felt they were getting somewhere," he says.

The maths work was too easy and the students were all getting 10 out of 10 but it kept them calm.

> "It was a key into the psyche of these young people. There was a balance to give them a level of success and a chance to be successful, where they couldn't in a normal mainstream school."

This group would have been throwing tables and chairs in a normal school. They sometimes did this in Ladywell. One defining observation for Graham was witnessing the demeanour of the home economics teacher, Winefride Hart, a wonderfully posh Glaswegian lady who was always impeccably dressed. This was a vital class in the school, partly because the pupils were able to consume the products of their work. This was often soups, mince and tatties, pizza, scones and biscuits. The pupils loved her and her classes and it was a perfect way to ensure pupils were getting proper nourishment.

> "This was a survival skill. This was like teaching someone who lives in the jungle how to use a hunting knife. Home economics was absolutely crucial," he says.

Graham learned from Winefride that teaching at this level was about getting as much 'under the radar' as you possibly can. He dubbed this the 'Ninja-style' of education where it is the life lessons underneath that are going to stick with the young person. One of Graham's more aggressive charges carved Possil gang initials into the desk with a banned pen knife. He proudly explained that 'PMS' stood for 'Possil Mad Skwad', and how it was daubed on their territory walls. Quietly spoken, Graham explained that PMS perhaps wasn't the best call sign when it referred to a women's menstrual cycle. Days later, the graffiti was changed to 'Possil Mad Team' or 'PMT'. Graham didn't have the heart to raise the matter a second time.

At Ladywell, he taught Office Information Studies, which revolved around basic administration in the workplace, and later this included computing skills. This was pretty ambitious for the average Ladywell pupil. One of the success stories was a boy called John [not his real name] who became a postman.

> "John was a violent and aggressive young man. Working in any way with the public was beyond contemplation. He was a deeply worrying person for us, although by no means the worst because several others ended up in prison for sexual assault. If he had a female teacher, he would often masturbate under the school desk. That was a serious worry… but this came with the territory and it was not unusual for people with mental health issues."

The school somehow managed to pacify this young man and steer him into an occupation where he was able to flourish and become a productive member of society. For teachers, it was all about listening to their pupils, which was never easy.

Winefride Hart's domain was her kitchen area in the basement, always finishing her lessons with a cup of tea and plate of Jammie Dodger biscuits for everyone. One afternoon, there was a commotion with crockery being smashed and pots and pans thrown on the floor. The work surfaces were being hammered and battered as one pupil called Thomas went on a rampage.

In what Philip Graham saw as a misguided approach to physical violence, Thomas's father had sent his son for lessons at a local boxing club.

> "All that does is turns a very violent young man into a very focused and violent young man, who knows how to use his violence. I have never believed that telling someone who is violent to redirect their violence, it is a big mistake. You are still not addressing the issue that violence is abhorrent."

He says children being encouraged to punch cushions and pillows is never an answer because it fosters the notion that the solution to any problem still involves violence.

> "Behind closed doors, does that produce an abuser in later years, I don't know. But I have never encouraged my children to think violence is ever the solution. If you feel violent, you need to sit down and talk about it. One thing for sure, you don't hit anything or anyone. A pillow is one thing, but then is it the cat, a small child, and in later

years is it a girl-friend, partner or wife?"

Thomas came pounding up the stairs and punched a perfect fist-shaped hole through a glass window reinforced with wire. If that had been a person's skull, there would have been serious damage. By now, Anne Bombelli was racing along the main corridor, and Philip Graham stepped out of his classroom, and the whole school was now in high anxiety with the pupils all excited by the drama. An agitated Winefride came running up the stairs.

"It's all my fault! It's my fault!" she exclaimed.

The head teacher looked at her quizzically.

"It's my fault. He told me last week he didn't like Jammie Dodgers and I gave him a plate of them."

Thomas went 'mental' because he had told Winefride he did not like Jammie Dodgers. His reaction was a test for a teacher in this situation. It was nothing to do with the biscuits. "He was saying 'You didn't listen to me'. And that's the most important thing for me now, is to be listened to," says Graham.

The devoted Winefride was distraught because she realised she had not been listening to Thomas. "*This boy had a strong reaction to being let down. For him, that reaction, is violent aggression,*" explains Graham. He points out the rational response to being let down is to be disappointed and upset, which is normal. How this is expressed is a spectrum with physical violence at the very negative end. It is the duty of educational professionals working in this charged environment to understand this.

He worked at Ladywell for eight years, earning about £18,000 to £20,000 a year, leaving before the school was closed as a day-school. In what can be seen as a short-sighted initiative, the Scottish Government were giving mainstream comprehensive schools funding for a Better Behaviour, Better Learning project, which was designed to bring the likes of John and Thomas back into the mainstream system, farming them out to Ladywell on certain week days and breaking the continuity.

"I don't buy that model at all. If you are trying to teach somebody, you need them to be with you. The idea that they could dip in for half days and made capable of sitting with their peers in a mainstream school does not work. You need to teach them *in situ* and arm the teachers with the correct skills and support or you take them out and admit they can't be in a class with 30 people," he says.

What Philip Graham explains here became the essence of the Newlands Junior College and was fully realised. A cohort of young people did not feel that they belonged to their schools, did not feel welcome and were therefore not managing to 'fit in'. Other educational interventions — great though they are in many respects — only take young people for part of the week and only for a few hours. Those young people are then expected to be able to fit back into school on their return, when they found it hard enough when they were there full time. When Newlands Junior College was created, it took young people in completely, full time and for good. The young people belonged to Newlands and Newlands belonged to them. Supportive adults in Newlands were there for them each and every week day. It was about solid and reliable relationships, which became like family.

Graham believes there is a broad spectrum of individuals who are attracted to a career in the teaching profession.

> "There are teachers who taught in Ladywell who couldn't go to St Aloysius and deliver an Advanced Higher course. There are people who would crumble under the parental pressure that would be brought to bear in a highly-academic atmosphere. Equally, there are teachers at St Aloysius, Hutchesons' Grammar School or Glasgow Academy, who would crumble in a place such as Ladywell. It is horses for courses, but there is no harm in that," he says.

He argues there is no such being as a 'universal great teacher' just as no two children are the same.

> "There are some teachers who are lucky enough to find their niche, although there are some teachers who think they have found their niche, and they are doing more harm than good."

Under the new arrangements at Ladywell, Philip Graham felt he could not properly deliver as a teacher and he moved on in March 2001.

......

The Govan High interview panel went swimmingly and Philip Graham landed a teaching job in a school 15 times larger than Ladywell. He and Iain White would begin a new chapter for the school, creating 'The Govan High Way'. Candidates for new posts were invited to spend the day at the school. After an initial hour or so spent with White, where, over tea or coffee in the conference room, he would explain how the school operated, its vision and *raison d'être*, a few pupils were invited in to speak with the candidates.

White would leave them alone. Often the expression on a candidate's face was one of blind panic. At the end of the school day, White would re-join the candidates. His attitude was if they were going to come and work, they had to be comfortable with the place and the pupils.

> "You've got to bring yourself to work, because if you don't then it's an act, and that's stressful. If you're having to put on a show every day as a teacher, it is not going to work," he says.

White advised candidates if they were not 100% up for it, then they should phone and say it was not for them. There was usually one or two who dropped out at this stage. In recruiting, White was really looking for educators with personality, gumption and flexibility, because he knew the Govan approach and the pace of change would frighten the life out of many teachers. Philip Graham was relatively immune to most behavioural issues. He looked across the table at White. "*OK, Iain, what is it you want me to do?*" said the fresh recruit. White smiled, leaned in like comedian Eric Morecombe, and then replied in his rich West of Scotland burr. "*I was rather hoping you were going to tell me, Philip.*"

The unorthodox interview style was an example of White's educational leadership style of 'facilitate and enable'.

> "The most significant thing we did at Govan was change the relationships we had, as professional educators, with young people. This was built up over time and coincided with Philip's arrival in developing a programme," explains White.

In his opening weeks, Graham made a staff presentation where he explained the kind of behaviourial culture he was aiming for. It was forged by his experience in an extreme educational environment. In Graham's view, Govan had a way to go because some staff were still on a path of change.

> "My experience in Ladywell had been presumptuous because the staff were all committed and bought into the theories of behaviour management and building relationships with young people. When I came to Govan I realised I wasn't going to be working with the young people as a priority, it was with the adults," says Graham.

While Govan's teachers needed some extra encouragement, Graham helped take the cultural change up a notch to the next level.

.....

Philip Graham's arrival in Govan came at a time when local and national politicians were turning their attention to the city's deep-seated social problems. Glasgow City Council began to invest in the area with an action plan for Central Govan in partnership with Scottish Enterprise, Communities Scotland, Greater Govan Social Inclusion Partnership and the Govan Initiative. The school decided to take a leaf from the pride and passion of Liverpool Football Club. Graham and White mirrored 'This is Anfield', a banner hanging above the players' tunnel as a reminder of who they were and what they were playing for, which helped exemplify the Liverpool legend, by adopting their own 'The Govan Way' and welcoming everyone who entered the school with the bold message: 'This is Govan High'. On White and Graham's departure to Newlands, it was quickly removed.

Philip Graham asked John Stevenson of Glasgow Creative, who worked with the school to get the same typeface as the Liverpool banner. This resonated with many of the football-loving pupils and it instilled a common sense of identity for many pupils. However, vital and pithy messaging requires constant re-affirmation, and this became the repetitive challenge for school leaders.

One chilly February morning Iain White wanted to know how many instances there had been since the beginning of the year of pupils being sent out for physical violence. Philip Graham consulted his meticulous notes on the computer and presented the figure.

"That's too many, get them all in the hall," he requested.

Half an hour later, the noise of 500 excitable pupils in the assembly hall created quite a buzz. White strode purposefully up to the front before turning round with a flourish. As he grimly faced the whole school, there was hush, and a pin dropping at the front would have been heard at the back. He launched into his topic. Usually, at his intermittent assemblies, he was full of praise for the achievements of everyone and always keen to encourage and pat his pupils on the back for their endeavour. This time his demeanour was more serious.

"I'm in here today, because I'm really disappointed. And I wanted to share my disappointment with you all. You know we don't allow you to hit one another in here. But since the New Year we've had far too many instances of people fighting. We're no havin' that. I'm no havin' that! You need to remember if you hit someone you'll be excluded from this school for the maximum period of time. It's a simple message and I know you can all understand it, so I hope you're taking it on board. Thanks very much."

Short and to the point and he began walking out past the rows of pupils in their seats. He was half way up when the clapping began and by the time he reached the back, it appeared 500 pupils were enthusiastically applauding the message. Andy Masterson, White's senior deputy head, was installed at the back door. *"There you are Iain, it doesnae get any better than this!"*

Govan's success was built on positive behaviour management. It was front and centre of everything, creating a place of safety and an environment for learning.

The Future Skills System was a neat invention at Govan High and it was built from scratch, with the help of the school's IT department and a third party contractor, Edict, based in the school. Phil Graham and his colleagues identified 76 discrete skills applicable to learning at school. These were skills that were not being recognised in the existing curriculum.

> "One of the skills was diagrammatic interpretation: the ability to look at a diagram and derive information from it. The maths teachers would all say they do this, and this is a problem because it becomes a subject silo at this point. Then the chemistry, biology, and geography teachers do it. Then the technical teachers will do it. Yet diagram information is being repeated all across the curriculum. It is not necessarily just a skill in maths, it's just a skill being taught in all these areas, in different ways," says Philip Graham.

The need to identify the 76 skills emerged from the interview techniques required to land a job. Typically, the opening question to make a candidate relax and which most candidates might knock out the park is: *'What are you good at?'* which leads to *'What skills can you bring to this organisation?'*

This was a ground-breaking approach with a Skills Assessment Booklet to assess each pupil, almost like a Myers-Briggs Type Indicator personality chart. The 76 skills were broken out into seven categories of skills, including the communicator, the do-er, the originator, the team-player and the trusted supporter. From the results, a pupil could clearly see where their strengths lay.

This unique system, explained and shown to HIME inspectors Carol McDonald and Elizabeth Morrison in September 2011, was offered to all secondary schools in Glasgow, yet the education department tried to shut it down. It transpired that Glasgow's Education Services directorate were already working on a parallel skills system with a company called Gateway. When Iain White inquired in the summer of 2009, whether the Gateway system would be ready by August. He was told "probably". It was still undelivered a decade later.

> "We also revamped the school's approach to focus on everybody getting into a positive destination rather than running the whole place for the small percentage who would go to university or higher education," he says.

This Govan-style approach would become a central tenet of Newlands Junior College.

One question concerned the kind of work destinations for pupils leaving the school. This involved asking: *what do young people want to be and do when they leave school?*

This is a hard question for most young persons to answer. Perhaps if they have professional parents who are doctors, lawyers, accountants, or teachers, they might have role models able to steer them towards the world of work, an expected lifestyle and what future remuneration might entail. Even for those working in a trade, such as a painter, an electrician, a joiner, hairdresser, or a beauty therapist, there is an element of understanding about the future of work and the prospects. But how does a young person learn to become a technical desktop draughtsman, an App programmer, a games developer, a banking investment 'quant', or any of the myriad of skilled jobs that have arrived as a result of the digital revolution in the last 20 years? Furthermore, if the parent or carer has no inkling about what kind of jobs are available, or how to even find out about them, what chance do those with a backdrop of generational unemployment?

Moreover, once a young person finds out what they want to be, what do they need in terms of qualifications and support to attain their goal and what does a school or a college need to provide?

At Govan High, the first step was organising a series of local Curriculum Conferences, which were facilitated by Kevin Sweeney, one of the deputy heads, who brought in an external consultant to pull it together. Parents and young people were invited along to hear from employers and from FE colleges and universities. The question was: "*What should we be doing here at the school?*"

In late 2005, armed with this feedback, White and his Leadership Team created a draft plan which they wanted to share with Ronnie O'Connor, then Glasgow's Director of Education. O'Connor would regularly meet with a group of Glasgow head teachers to chew the fat about education. Towards the Christmas holidays, White drafted a single page of A4 and sent it for O'Connor's consideration. In essence, it was about streamlining the curriculum, removing certain peripheral subjects, and replacing it with new elements of study and many more experiences of the world of work. O'Connor's response was swift and he wanted to learn more. The plan was about ending the age and stage of pupils, with all pupils making their option choices at the end of S1. This was a radical change from other Scottish schools. All pupils would choose six Standard Grades (or the equivalents such as Intermediate level I/II, Access or a Pre-vocational courses) to be studied over a two-year period. This all depended on the number of teaching periods per week. There were 30 defined periods each week. Each Standard grade would be allocated five periods a week, significantly more than the three periods per subject.

> "This will *not* be more time to go slower. As this is significantly more than the three periods at present, departments have already identified what would be added to the present course to enhance motivation, improve attainment levels at Standard Grade, gain additional certification, and to widen the view and strengthen the link with the world of work," said the note.

In the early New Year, O'Connor joined the Leadership Team for the first of three two-hour long sessions, where O'Connor, despite the freezing January temperatures, took off his jacket and rolled up his sleeves.

> "Over the past ten years the school has progressively moved towards a core skills and work-related approach for its young people largely through enterprise and leadership experiences," stated the note. [42]

The group thrashed out what was entailed with O'Connor. The Govan High staff were all consulted, while pupils and parents were invited to discuss the proposals at several assemblies. All of the stakeholders were in broad agreement and supported the proposals. The five extra periods in the 30-period week would be used for core physical education, one of religious and moral education, and two other periods for the personal and social development

---

42 New Curricular Structure, Proposals for Executive Director (Education, Training and Young People), Govan High School, April 2006.

of the pupil, giving them practical experiences of the world of work. At the end of this two-year period, pupils would move onto a one-year course at Intermediate of equivalent with some pupils leaving school at the end of S4 with five Standard Grades and five other certificates at Intermediate level or the equivalent.

> "It is a major aim of this school to prepare young people for the world of work providing them with both the academic qualifications and soft skills required to gain employment. To this end the revised curricular structure will build on and further develop current good practice both 'in-house' and working with partner agencies," said the proposal.

White recalls: "We made these curriculum changes and we improved the skills base for young people building this prevocational structure. We created far more vocationally-slanted experiences for the young people. We partnered with local Further Education (FE) colleges and various other providers to deliver courses and we got permission from Ronnie O'Connor to ignore the guidelines that were in place from the Scottish Education Department."

In April 2006, Andy Masterson and White were sent for by O'Connor and they were surprised to meet the whole Glasgow Education Services senior team, where they were encouraged to explain their radical proposition. White was anxious to get the timetable approved, formalise the options for pupils and parents, ready to the start of the new term in August 2007. The new approach also required some extra teaching resources, especially in teaching English. They were quizzed by the executive group and then given the green light to go ahead.

In 2007, when Scottish Government officials in Edinburgh heard what was going on, they were unhappy that National Curriculum guidelines appeared to be being flaunted. Several heavy-hitting school inspectors descended on Govan High to ensure that the guidelines were not being breached. White was viewed as arrogant and conceited when he informed one school inspector that guidelines were there for guidance and it was up to the head teacher to decide when and how they could be applied.

> "If your guidelines don't meet the needs and aspirations of the community here, then I don't need to follow them, and that's why we're *no* following them," he declared bluntly.

The statistics spoke for the success. When White arrived at Govan, only 4% of pupils went on into further or higher education. The school had a higher number of young people in the NEET category than almost any other school in Scotland. By the time he left, the total was up to 17%, with many more moving into Modern Apprenticeship schemes. Maureen McKenna, by now the Director of Education, asked White what he thought of the exam results at Govan High.

> "Since there are 11 criterion in which we are judged and Govan improved in nine of them, and remained steady in the other two, I think we can be pretty happy with the way things are going," he replied.

Another initiative was the Graduate Programme, set up by Graham Robertson, who would later become Newlands' Principal Teacher of Careers and Guidance. Robertson was the architect of this special programme to help encourage disadvantaged young people to consider going to university. White had been perturbed when he found out the school's Dux, who had secured a fine set of Highers in her exams, was going to undertake a Higher National Certificate (HNC) for a year, then a two-year Higher National Diploma (HND) and then enter the third year of a business course at university, before graduation with honours. He inquired why she opted for this perfectly acceptable, yet convoluted, pathway when she had been more than capable of going straight into first year at university. "*I didnae think university was for folk like me,*" she told White. He went back to see Robertson where they discussed how and why capable young people in Govan still lacked the self-confidence to choose a university education.

Under Govan's auspices, Robertson developed another programme to build self-belief in young people. Robertson had been trained as a facilitator for The Pacific Institute (TPI), which provides training in positive psychology. The Pacific Institute took on the challenges of education in the United States. In November 2002, President Bush enacted the No Child Left Behind Act, which demanded a higher-level of performance from students around the country. The No Child Left Behind Act mandated that 100% of all students must receive passing scores on state administered tests by 2014. Teachers asked how could this be achieved. Principals from schools began attending a two-day training of TPI's 21 Keys for High Performance Teaching and Learning curriculum. TPI worked with teachers and the positive impacts were significant, particularly in maths and reading scores. The results ignited Robertson's interest. At the end of their second year, a group of 20 bright young people in Govan were invited into a personal development programme called *The Graduate*. For a week near the end of the summer term, the 'graduates' were given a lot of tasks and then the best would be judged. Robertson based

The Graduate on the BBC TV's series *The Apprentice* with Iain White acting as Lord Sugar. This was just a fun part of their wider PSE programme, which included tours of universities from Cambridge through to Sunderland to see what was on offer across the university spectrum. One of this cohort, Jennifer Baird, managed to obtain a first class honours in mathematics from University of Glasgow. Sadly, when Robertson left Govan High to join Newlands, they immediately disbanded his programme.

The good news for Newlands was Robertson had amassed considerable experience with The Pacific Institute which became a hallmark of the junior college's success story. At Newlands, one of the major policy drivers was GIRFEC (Getting It Right for Every Child and Young Person), a national Scottish Government policy which was enhanced by Robertson's involvement with the strategy at Govan.

......

All of this was relevant background which helped inform the educational development of Newlands Junior College. By the end of June 2014, Iain White had made a number of appointments at Newlands, while the search was going on to fill the science post. This allowed the successful applicants to hand in their notice to their schools.

Controversially, White's sparring partner was about to join the project too. In his final interview for the position of Depute Principal at the College, Philip Graham was asked to draft a speech.

> *"Your Principal has been given a short slot at a Glasgow head teachers' meeting to explain how Newlands Junior College will offer a worthwhile alternative for some young people without undermining the mainstream school system. Several of the heads are known to be sceptical. At the last minute a message was received saying that the Principal's car has broken down and that you will have to deliver the speech in his place."*

On 23rd June 2014, Graham jotted down his thoughts for a seven-minute response. From all accounts, he did exceptionally well and was offered the job. It should have been a red letter day achievement. But it soon developed into a nasty spat. That evening, he sat down and penned his letter of resignation. Next day, Tuesday, 24th June 2014, he delivered his resignation letter by hand to his line manager at Govan High School. White and Graham began to meet to discuss how the college would work. It was a sharing of their beliefs and what this bold and uncharted venture would be like. It meant several snatched meetings at Caffè Nero in Union Street, opposite the side entrance to Central Station and a convenient spot for the train from Gourock, and a ten-minute drive from Govan High School. It was here, over numerous flat white coffees, that a joint vision for the college's daily operation was forged.

However, the obstruction emanating from Education Services became deeply personal, with not-unreasonable concerns that the appointments would leave a serious hole in Govan High's senior leadership. The Director of Education met with White and Bloomer and demanded to see the whole curriculum before she would sanction pupils being allowed to go from any Glasgow schools. She wanted details of every course that was to be taught, all the resources that would be used, and the teachers' plans for a full two-year course.

> "It was an absolutely farcical demand. As a head teacher, I would never have made this demand of any teaching colleagues in my schools. And it was a demand that the Director of Education had never made on any other school teacher in Glasgow. But we had to work with her at the time, so we did it. We prepared all the information which was requested," says White.

The Education Services directorate appeared to misunderstand the junior college's rationale. The junior college would be working with individuals who had been challenged by the existing system, and the strategy was to be flexible and responsive to each individual student's requirements, not prescriptive about courses and timetables set in stone.

> "We would have to roll with the punches and change our approach on the ground as we found it," says White.

The new Principal's view was the Education Services department deliberately put unnecessary hurdles in place to stymie the development of his establishment. But there was another blast at the college and Philip Graham remains shocked by the response as he decided to join White at Newlands. Graham's resignation, as another leaver from Govan High School, created a stink in Education Services and a question arose over whether the summer holiday period could be included in Graham's six-week notice period. He received a letter for Glasgow City Council on 25 August 2014 about his exit, saying he was breaking his contracts.

> *"I am writing to express my disappointment at the manner in which you have left Govan High School. Your notice period was eight weeks*

and you did not hand in your resignation until the second last day of term before the summer break. Councils have always taken teachers' notice period to be eight weeks of term time, although I appreciate that SNCT [43] is silent on this matter." [44]

McKenna stated Govan High was left with an acting head teacher, one substantive depute head teacher and one acting depute head teacher which was why the council wanted Graham to work his full notice period. *"Your leaving in this manner suggests a level of disregard for the needs of the school and your former colleagues."* She concluded: *"I would normally write to thank colleagues moving on for their service to the city as I am always very appreciative of the work of staff who go the extra mile for the good of our young people. I am sorry that I do not feel that I can say this for you."*

Certainly, there were now senior staff vacancies to be filled at Govan High which was a serious headache, but McKenna emailed White complaining: *"I am particularly concerned as the role as Deputy Principal will potentially involve him liaising with Glasgow schools when he has shown such little regard to the continuity of education of Govan's young people. It does not bode well for positive relationships with the Council."* [45]

If Philip Graham was not to be allowed to leave Govan until after the October break, it would prevent the opening of the junior college in time for the autumn term. Graham found the letter from the education department "grotesquely personal" and, as it was copied to Keir Bloomer, it displayed an "ignorance of data protection". The Educational Institute of Scotland's area representative Alan Scott stepped in to help Graham, with Amanda Jones, a seasoned employment lawyer with Maclay Murray & Spens, offering her opinion.

> *"Amanda is clear, that Mr Graham is entitled to rely on the terms of his contract and leave. Short of the Council raising an interdict to stop him going Mr Graham can leave at the expiry of his due notice,"* a note from the EIS to Alan Scott stated.

There was a further note from Scott to Education Services. *"Under section 14.2.1 of the SNCT Handbook, Mr Graham is required to provide you with eight weeks' notice, I understand from Mr Graham that he hand delivered his*

---

43 SNCT is the national negotiating body representing COSLA, the Convention of Scottish Local Authorities, the Scottish Government, and the teaching trade unions in Scotland. The SNCT handbook sets out conditions of service for teachers.
44 Letter to Philip Graham from Glasgow Education Services, August 2014.
45 Email from Maureen McKenna to Iain White, 22 August 2014.

resignation letter to his line manager on Tuesday 24 June 2014. It appears that you have misinterpreted section 14.2.4 of the SNCT Handbook. This section allows each party to give longer period of notice than the minimum period they are required to provide. It does not allow you to unilaterally increase the minimum period of notice Mr Graham is obliged to provide you with. For the avoidance of doubt Mr Graham has asked me to indicate to you that his last working day will be Tuesday 19ᵗʰ August 2014. In so doing I am clear that he has complied with his obligation to you under the terms of the contract."

Graham consulted his brother, who was also a lawyer. His advice was to write to express his disappointment at the tone of the letter. Diplomatically, and for the sake of his new employer, Graham decided not to pursue this issue, but the matter was clearly a symptom of a festering relationship. He took up his new post on 20ᵗʰ August 2014.

The bad blood between the Education Service directorate and Newlands teaching recruits filtered through the city's education system. Back at Govan High, the Future Skills System, previously lauded as exemplary, was dismantled by the new head teacher with agreement from the Director of Education's office. Any well of goodwill towards Newlands Junior College was at a low ebb.

There is a valid argument that Iain White and Newlands Junior College, in selecting several key staff from a single school, made an error of judgement when there appeared to be suitable applicants from a wider pool.

After the summer break, the new faces gathered at Newlands. Samantha Wrigglesworth as the English teacher, the Mathematics teacher was Douglas Clark, who later took students off to try playing rugby, and science teacher Kenny McDonald, who had been head of sciences at Govan High School. This poured further petrol on the fire with Education Services as White was seen as poaching colleagues from his old place of work. Iain White shrugged off the complaints and pressed on with his team-building.

> "We had the opportunity to get the team and envision what this place was going to be like and how it would operate. Most importantly, in my view, we set out what our culture was going to be like for the young people."

An admired educational consultant, Cathy Ota, was brought up from Brighton, and worked with the new staff as a facilitator helping to pull together different ideas.

94

In addition to the teachers, Billy Huxter, a Skill Force instructor who had served in the British Armed Forces, joined to help with the personal development of the students. After academic and vocational, personal development was the third leg of the Newlands Junior College stool.

This would involve physical, health and motivational experiences, linking up with the Duke of Edinburgh Awards Scheme, with students preparing for and undertaking the programme over two academic years, leading to the Bronze Duke of Edinburgh award. The Bronze award has four sections including volunteering, physical, skills and expedition and each person must undertake a minimum of three months' activity in each of the categories. This culminated in a two-day expedition involving an over-night stay in a tent or similar temporary structure.

The Duke of Edinburgh Award had been viewed as the preserve of private education and middle-class pupils across the UK, but its Extending the Reach programme was addressing this perception and wanted to include students from places such as Newlands. Tackling these awards proved to be one of the most exhilarating experiences and a pinnacle of physical achievements for many Newlands students. It exposed young inner-city students to the Great Outdoors, to local countryside with forest walks and seaside trips, and to farming and the natural landscape. Huxter's role was to provide leadership and guidance for the young people helping them achieve ASDAN (Award Scheme Development and Accreditation Network) Personal Development, SQA Level 3 Employability, Health & Safety, and First Aid. ASDAN awards were also recognised by the university entrance system, UCAS.

With the finishing touches being applied to the Minto Building, the summer weeks before students arrived allowed the team to gather in situ and bond well.

> "The opportunity to have everyone together before the arrival of the students was really good for us. It gave us a belief and a passion for what we were undertaking. Nobody had ever done this before. We were about to take young people who had disengaged from the education system, from different schools around the south side of Glasgow, and bring them together in one place," says White.

Wellbeing extended to the nutritional requirements for each student, many coming from homes where there was little nourishing food on the table. So making sure the students were able to have breakfast and lunch became a critical factor and canteen manager Mary Rossi and canteen assistant Caroline

Turnbull were integrated into the staff team and played important roles in 'feeding' the college's culture.

> "I was in industrial catering, where I was working mostly with male adults. I came to NJC [Newlands Junior College] to help out for a few weeks and have never left. In those first few weeks I really enjoyed working with the students, especially when they started to call me Aunty Mary, which made me feel part of the family and not just a cog in a machine," says Mary.

The team had a clear mission: the young people coming to the junior college had not been getting their entitlement out of the school system in Glasgow. At Newlands, that would be rectified.

> "This was not because schools are intrinsically bad places in themselves — they are not — but they just don't suit everybody. Our job was to take this new group and help them. Our desire was to make a difference for these young people," says White.

There was an urgency and vitality which galvanised the team and this energy was able to rub off on those who walked through the door.

> "The whole college was put together in a remarkably short period of time. It was a timescale a local authority could never have hoped to match," says White.

NEWLANDS JUNIOR COLLEGE (2014-2019)

On the Cover:
Shania Ashraf, Megan Preston, Aimee McCambridge help with the promotion of the Newlands Junior College Yearbook in 2017.

Class Acts: Bernard Moffat, Marc Kerr and Kyle McCrae. Special thanks to photographer Martin Shields for use of pictures.

Making it Happen: Jim McColl, the founder, and Iain White, the Principal of Newlands Junior College, make a public announcement about the junior college's foundation in 2014.
Picture courtesy: The Scotsman Publications.

THE BEGINNING OF A MISSION

Welcome to the Junior College:
The Minto Building, a former industrial training facility, on the south side of Glasgow, was transformed into a modern place of learning where the junior college students felt a 'sense of belonging'.

Early Days:
Jim McColl speaks with the first cohort of junior college students and explains his hopes for the young people. He said later: "The key to the junior college's success was to get the young people out of the environment they were in because they were being failed in that environment. Getting them into their own environment, nurturing them and engaging them was critical to the success of Newlands Junior College."

Opening Time:
Jim McColl on the STV News in October 2014 explaining his delight at the junior college's opening.

THE VISIT OF NICOLA STURGEON, SCOTLAND'S FIRST MINISTER, 18 MARCH 2016

Welcome for a VIP:
Principal Iain White discusses the work and activities of Newlands Junior College with Nicola Sturgeon, Scotland's First Minister, during her visit on 18th March 2016. Junior college students Chris Baillie and Edward Pert join the First Minister for lunchtime sandwiches.

Pictures to Cherish:
Nicola Sturgeon, Scotland's First Minister, hears from students about life at the junior college and agrees to have a 'selfie' taken with a delighted Megan Lynch, which she shares with Jim McColl.

THE LIFE-CHANGING ENDEAVOUR OF NEWLANDS JUNIOR COLLEGE

Colour coding:
Highlighter pens proved to be a handy aid for students sharing their work.

Laptop success:
Students at Newlands Junior College enjoyed personal access to the latest learning technologies, including the popular Apple Mac laptops.

HAPPINESS
IS A CUP OF COFFEE

Newlands Junior College
Community Coffee Morning

Friday 15th December 2017
10:30am – 12:00 pm
6 Inverlair Avenue, Cathcart,
Glasgow G43 2HS

NEWLANDS JUNIOR COLLEGE

RSVP: newlandsjcommunitycouncil@gmail.com
or call: 0141 212 4477

Local heroes:
The coffee morning, instigated and run by Newlands Junior College students in December 2017, was an initiative which helped build strong community bonds with the neighbourhood.

Sunshine on heath:
Conor Payling (left), Nathan Crichton and William Clark step out together on a summer trek in the hills.

On the lab bench:
Science experimentation was a key part of the learning programme for students.

The Great Outdoors:
A snack break for a group of students out in the hills during preparations to undertake their Duke of Edinburgh's Award schemes.

Transport of delight:
The daily minibus was an integral part of a student's life, picked up and dropped off near their homes. Pictured are TJ Bonner (left), Alistair Elder and Charlie McBride.

THE LIFE-CHANGING ENDEAVOUR OF NEWLANDS JUNIOR COLLEGE

Workplace visitors:
Newlands Junior College students shown around the Poppy Scotland factory, where they met armed forces veterans now working with the national charity in March 2016. Workplace visits were a popular and regular aspect of student life.

Scotland the Brave:
Jamie Barbour pipes a welcome to the Newlands Junior College's First Graduation Ceremony, held at Hampden Park, the National Football Stadium, Glasgow, in June 2016.

NEWLANDS JUNIOR COLLEGE GRADUATION IN 2018, (CITY OF GLASGOW COLLEGE)

Prize guys:
Peter Gordon (applauding centre), Daniel Medford (front second right), Daniel McClafferty
(front first right), among the audience of students, staff, parents and carers at the Newlands Junior College's
Graduation Ceremony in City of Glasgow College in 2018.

Class of 2018:
The Newlands Junior College group picture of the year with Philip Graham and Iain White.
Pictures: Martin Shields.

THE LIFE-CHANGING ENDEAVOUR OF NEWLANDS JUNIOR COLLEGE

Class of 2019:
The final cohort of Newlands Junior College graduates with the Principals in June 2019.

Certificates of success:
Students Josh Stewart, Lisa Kane, Daniel McClafferty and Marc Kerr received their awards during the graduation ceremony in June 2019 from Alex Stewart, Jim McColl and Phil Carr, the SkillForce instructor.

Well done to all:
Jay O'Malley, Carly Redmond, Daniel Medford and Ross McArthur collect their scrolls and certificates during the graduation ceremony in June 2019.

NEWLANDS JUNIOR
—
COLLEGE

Eye to Eye:
Philip Graham congratulates Bernard Moffat on his junior college success at the June 2019 ceremony.

SHARING THE PLEASURE OF JUNIOR COLLEGE SUCCESS

Josh Stewart celebrates his success with his grandmother Caroline after the Newlands Junior College Graduation in June 2019.

Ross McArthur and his parents, Kenny and Linda, at the Newlands Junior College Graduation in June 2019.

NEWLANDS JUNIOR COLLEGE

Lisa Kane with her Aunty, Helen Macduff, at the Newlands Junior College Graduation in June 2019.

Truck stop: Malcolm Group, the national logistics and transportation company, hosted Jim McColl and junior college students at their Brookfield depot and headquarters with Scotland rugby star Al Kellock. From left: Megan Lynch, Jim McColl, Edan Harley, Al Kellock, Megan Donnelly, Andrew Malcolm and Paul Simpson. Directors Andrew and Walter Malcolm were generous supporters of the junior college.

PRIDE IN THEIR ACHIEVEMENTS

Fine Achievement:
Carol Henry, the People Director of Arnold Clark, presents a certificate to Nathan O'Brian at the graduation ceremony.

Handshake of delight:
Kieran Just receives his scroll from Philip Graham during the Newlands Junior College graduation ceremony in City of Glasgow College in 2018.

Success stories:
Shania Ashraf (top) with Jim McColl, Marci Patterson (centre) with Sheila Lodge,
the Depute Principal of City of Glasgow College; and Ross McArthur with Jim McColl,
at the 2018 graduation.

THE INSPIRING JUNIOR COLLEGE STAFF

Master of Science: Kenny McDonald, a popular figure with students.

Staff First XI:
The Newlands Junior College team in 2019: (back row) Kenny McDonald, Chris Devlin, Douglas Clark, Phil Carr and Donald Macleod. (Front row) Caroline Turnbull, Elizabeth Orenes, Philip Graham, Iain White, Rachel Buchanan and Mary Rossi.

Ex-Navy veteran: Phil Carr, the SkillForce and outdoor instructor.

Mentor:
Alex Stewart,
deputy chair of
the junior college
trustees.

Numbers man:
Douglas Clark,
mathematics teacher
and rugby fan.

THE THANKS AND APPRECIATION OF SUPPORTERS

In listening mode:
Supporters of the Newlands
Junior College way: former
students Edan Harley, now an
'ambassador' for the work of
the college, and Paul Simson.

Key partnership:
Douglas Clark presents an
award to Carol Henry, the
People Director of Arnold Clark,
celebrating the company's support
of the junior college.

Elizabeth Stewart, the wife of Alex Stewart, deputy chair of the trustees, enjoys a moment of fun at the junior college graduation. The Stewarts were generous supporters of the junior college with Alex becoming a mentor to many young people.

Nice set of wheels: Qasim Bilal, who graduated from Newlands Junior College in 2016 and secured an apprenticeship with Arnold Clark, shows off his motorbike to Kenny McDonald.

Thank you:
Lisa Kane, now an 'ambassador' for the work of the junior college, presents a bouquet of flowers to Gillian Hunt, educational consultant and supporter of Newlands Junior College.

Below left:
The Pure Pleasure of Achievement: Jim McColl, Iain White and guests enjoy a lighter moment during the graduation ceremony.

Below centre:
Movin' and Groovin': Marci Patterson, Margaret Carmichael and Peter Gordon celebrate after the formal procedures on graduation day are over.

Below right:
All Eyes to the Front: A view of the Newlands Junior College Graduation ceremony at the City of Glasgow College in 2018.

Moments to savour: Peter Gordon, who has since become an 'ambassador' for the work of Newlands Junior College, shares his joy during the graduation ceremony in 2018. After Newlands, his 'positive destination' resulted in a Modern Apprenticeship with Arnold Clark, one of the college's major supporters and private sector funders.

THE PRINCIPAL AND VICE PRINCIPAL

NEWLANDS JUNIOR
—
COLLEGE

Driving force: Iain White, the Newlands Junior College Principal, said: "We really moved the junior college forward. We had an emphasis on meeting the needs and aspirations of every single child, whether they were aspiring to a university career or entering directly into the world of work. The real bottom line for us – as far as we possibly could - was to get every young person that left us into a positive destination." Picture courtesy: Times Educational Supplement Scotland (TESS).

Setting the standard: Philip Graham, the Depute Newlands Junior College Principal, said in describing how the junior college managed to build trust and confidence. "If you sweat the small stuff — such as gently dealing with issues such as wearing the wrong kind of trousers — then the big stuff doesn't become an issue."

CHAPTER TWELVE:
The Arrival of the First Cohort

Anxious. Nervous. Apprehensive. Filled with trepidation. Every new junior college student was trying to overcome an array of daunting feelings, clinging to a hope that perhaps this alien place might change the course of their lives. So who exactly were the young people about to embark on an adventurous chapter in their lives?

For the trustees a primary issue was identifying the most suitable individuals for the college. Trustee Eddie Hawthorne, the head of Arnold Clark, wants to be clear about why he backed the junior college.

> "The way that Jim and Alex explained it to me and how it came about with Iain and Philip as the principal and deputy principal needs to be understood. A lot of people concluded that Newlands was taking 'problem children'. No, they were not. They were not problem children or young people at all. These were people who were not engaged in mainstream education or they were having issues in their personal life that was preventing them attending a mainstream school. These were, in my opinion, issues that were stopping them maximising their education," he says. [46]

As head of admissions, Philip Graham was on the look-out for the right group for the first cohort.

> "My first contact with all of the students was through the Nomination Form, which we received from the schools. Three of us in the admissions team would go through these forms and look for indications from the schools of a bit of 'spark' from the young persons," says Graham.

His team were also alert to any 'red flags' which suggested the applicant was simply not the right fit for Newlands.

> "If they had a catastrophically low attendance rate, it was unlikely that we, as a bunch of strangers as we would be to the young people, would be able to turn this around easily. We did take some people with really low attendance rates, but there were real mitigating circumstances. If the Nomination Form seemed to fit the profile, we would set up an interview and meet the prospective student face to face."

46 Interview with the author, January 2020.

There were Glasgow teachers who were open-minded enough to find out more. One was a Deputy Head Teacher at Holyrood Secondary School, Margaret Leyden, who retired from teaching in 2018.

> "The deputy head was absolutely terrific to Newlands. She was one of the very few deputy heads who came and visited. She sat down, talked to us and tried to work out what we were like. She tried to find out who we were as people, what services we offered. She was positive, open-minded but healthily and encouragingly sceptical," says Graham.

Such was the relationship that a seminar for parents and carers to raise awareness was co-presented by Holyrood Secondary and the school worked on developing week-long assessments for potential Newlands nominees rather than a single day. Many applicants, recruited at the end of S2 and aged about 14, simply wanted out of their existing Glasgow school surroundings.

> "The usual interview focused on the problems each applicant was having at school. Some applicants felt all their issues would be sorted by coming away from those problems. In a lot of our interviews, you got the impression that the person didn't care if they were going to a garden shed or Newlands Junior College, as long as they were getting away from their school," says Graham.

Nevertheless, the continuing attrition from within Education Services prevented the new college from going into more schools and speaking with potential students. Moreover, the fledgling institution was not allowed to hand out 'marketing' materials to young people or their parents and carers.

> "It [the Education Services department] seemed to want to focus on keeping information away from parents and what might be available to them," says Graham.

All nominations had to be made through joint assessment teams in the schools. The behaviour of some head teachers in Glasgow schools was deeply discourteous, and meetings were described by Newlands staff as, at best, "*rude*" and, at worst, as "*positively hostile*".

Senior teaching staff at Shawlands Academy, St Margaret Mary's in Castlemilk, and King's Park Secondary, were all viewed as hostile to the Newlands concept. One trustee had been a pupil at a Glasgow south side secondary and thought this might be a good introduction to speak about Newlands but the head teacher declined the opportunity. When the trustee sent a charitable donation to the school's appeal for extra-curricular funds, it was returned without comment.

Another head teacher was so embarrassed by the behaviour of their colleagues that they privately apologised to Iain White and Keir Bloomer after a particularly rumbustious session. The unambiguous signal from several head teachers who chose not to engage was their implied disapproval of McColl and private sector involvement in education.

> "For those head teachers who didn't want anything to do with us, it might have been a fundamental issue or against their principles because it was outside the public sector, but these heads really need to take a long hard look in the mirror and ask themselves, 'What happened to the young people that we didn't nominate? What lives do they have right now?'" asks Stewart. "We were not child snatchers going around playgrounds pulling kids out like *Chitty Chitty Bang Bang*. That never happened. All of the nomination process was through the local authority, so they had identified themselves that these young people needed the help from Newlands, it was head teachers who did this," he says.

In spite of the rancour, the big day arrived on Monday, 20th October 2014. And it was special for so many people, including Jim McColl and Alex Stewart who were ready to welcome the first intake. Nothing compared with that genuine mix of expectation and trepidation as the first students arrived and made their way through the front door. The former Minto Building's ground floor was now in mint condition, the freshly-painted walls were adorned with inspirational messages, the out-of-the-box computers plugged in, the workstations clean and clear, and the aroma of sizzling sausages [healthier foods were gently introduced] permeating from the canteen, ready for the arrival of 30 nervous young people.

What mattered most was the welcome from Iain, Philip and the team. Every one of the new arrivals was as special as any royalty – VIPs in their own right. The first day was spent getting to know each of the students and explaining to them the ethos and culture. It must be underlined that at the time of their admission, all students were at risk of educational failure, and around 70% of students came from homes in the most disadvantaged quintile of the Scottish Index of Multiple Deprivation (SIMD).

> "We made it clear that this was their junior college and we would do everything we could to help them, but that they must also be willing and prepared to put in the effort. We would do our very best for them and ensure that they were given opportunities to show what they could achieve for themselves," says White.

As an educator, Philip Graham says it was a privilege to be involved at the start of such a progressive idea.

"Before the doors opened, the whole place looked immaculate and what it needed was the buzz of the young people. Their arrival brought the whole place to life in an instant. It was remarkable," he recalls.

It was transformational for young people such as Matthew, who was an anonymous case study in Gillian Hunt's report of the college.

"Matthew says that when he started at Newlands it was like a switch going on. The atmosphere was completely different. He says that he was recently looking at photos of him with other NJC students from that year and he looked so happy, that he belonged." [47]

Induction and team relationship building took up the first weeks at Newlands. This formed a strong base for Matthew and the other students.

"Matthew says that the college showed him that teaching can be done differently and that his time there taught him to 'put the work in'. He states that, at school, teachers had to help you but at Newlands teachers wanted to help you. As many other students have said, Matthew believes that he was treated as an equal by the adults at Newlands." [48]

Trustee Scott Black acknowledges that these vital few days and weeks set a precise tone. *"Iain, Philip and all the staff did a great job of bringing the building to life."* Only a few days after the opening, the runes were good. On Thursday 6th November, Philip Graham emailed school colleagues: *"Just a quick note to let you know that the pupil(s) selected from your school to join Newlands Junior College have made a spectacularly positive start. Everyone has arrived, settled in, had breakfast and is off completing tasks."* [49]

The following Friday, 14th November, Graham sent another upbeat update. *"All pupils have settled well and are engaged with their coursework. I will shortly be sending out information on our reporting system, so that you will be able to track the progress of your former pupils at NJC."*

Graham encouraged the head teachers to follow the Facebook pages and Twitter feeds to keep a track of their former pupils and signed off saying.

"You should feel free to come and visit us – we would be only too delighted to give

---

47 NJC 2014-2019 Report, Gillian Hunt, 2020.
48 Ibid, Gillian Hunt, 2020.
49 Philip Graham emails to Glasgow schools nominating students, November 2014.

you a tour! If you think it would be helpful for potential candidates to see the college, that can be easily arranged too."

Sometimes, it was a slow burn getting young people into the Newlands way.

According to Gillian Hunt:

> "Finn [not his real name] started Newlands and there was no immediate epiphany. His attendance was not great and those first few months were a bit bumpy!"

The student responded: "It's not like you go from school, then you go to Newlands and you're perfect…but the main thing is relationships with the teachers … you start to develop better behaviours."

> "Finn believes that he had learned little in two and a half years at secondary school. Staff at NJC, and Finn, discovered that he was a really bright young man, in his first year passing National 4 in English, maths and engineering science and in his second year National 5 in maths, practical electronics and computer games development. In addition he secured many vocational and personal development qualifications," says the report.

Finn picked up a number of awards on his graduation, but the prize he and his Gran were probably most proud of was the one for 100% attendance.

Not everyone fitted into the new college. Several young people came along and tried to settle in but for various reasons, they decided to return to their secondary schools, where the positive outcomes for such candidates remains unclear.

> "That first year was one of incredible learning for everyone. It was a steep curve. We had to be adaptive and change things on a daily basis. We were responding day by day to how everyone was fitting in and we watched with amazement the transformation of so many young people. This was what made us excited to come in to work every day. Certainly, we had lots of issues to deal with – including some major behavioural ones where we said what was acceptable, but the young people knew they were being treated fairly and with respect," recalls Iain White.

In June 2015, the first full session of Newlands drew to a satisfactory close. There was an unbelievable sense of completing an arduous and tricky journey together. The work of every student was recognised, and they prepared to return for their second year. Student Megan Lynch sang beautifully during the afternoon celebration where Jim McColl and Iain White mingled with many family members, partners and friends of the college.

> "The atmosphere was just brilliant with an air of excitement, achievement and happiness being really evident. It was an excellent way to round off what had been a terrific opening session for all of us." [50]

50 NJC, Progress Report, No3. August 2015.

CHAPTER THIRTEEN:
How to Change a Young Person's Self-Image

Educational psychologists once pontificated about a particular Scottish problem: an inherent lack of self-esteem among Scots. They blamed this for holding people back from achieving more with their lives. In the early years of the 21ˢᵗ century, it had become a central plank in improving the wellbeing of the nation. Philip Graham had become deeply involved with educational development and met with a senior psychologist called Peter Sheridan. This was about sharing best practice and techniques around self-esteem and it developed Graham's intellectual interest. He undertook a post-graduate diploma in support for learning at St Andrew's College, under the wing of the University of Glasgow.

> "This was during the big self-esteem fad of the mid-1990s when everybody was talking about boosting self-esteem and everyone should be focusing on boosting self-confidence," he says.

Carol Craig's *The Scots' Crisis of Confidence*, [51] was one of the popular books which tackled this subject, pointing out that *"self-esteem is similar to self-confidence but gives more weight to feelings of self-worth than to self-efficacy"*. Her thesis was that if a person lacks self-confidence and feels useless or hopeless, then they may succumb to a "victim mentality" or over-compensate by acting in an arrogant or bullying manner. Philip Graham reckons Carol Craig's thesis was one of the better contributions to the debate about why Scots were reticent and not performing as well.

> "Doing my research, I had to completely change the direction. Because I had been constantly told that children with social and emotional behavioural difficulties had these issues because they had very low self-esteem," he says.

Yet this was not what Graham's research concluded when he undertook a series of surveys measuring esteem among a cohort of young people in the West of Scotland with social, emotional or behavioural challenges.

> "Their self-esteem was sky high. Absolutely sky-high," he says.

51 The Scots' Crisis of Confidence, Carol Craig, Published by Big Thinking, 2003.

Perplexed, he consulted one of his lecturers saying this did not compute with the received wisdom. Was this a 'false-positive' with young people presenting as having high self-esteem because one of the factors of low self-esteem was a propensity to exaggerate and act out exuberant behaviour?

Graham was encouraged to follow his line of research. He asked more questions which backed up his new proposition. Young people did indeed have very high self-esteem, which was genuine. However, this was all to do with their self-image and where they saw themselves in comparison with their immediate peer group.

> "A young person's self-esteem is regularly boosted by significant people in their life, usually a parent, a mother or a father. If they say you are good at something, this is an opinion that you really value. If a parent says you are bad at something, this is crushing," he says.

So if a young person's father is in Barlinnie Jail in Glasgow for stealing cars, their self-esteem may well be measured on how well they can break into a vehicle. If you commit this crime, escape getting caught and stay out of prison, your self-esteem is going to be sky-high. This is because the self-image is of being a thief or a criminal.

> "If you are involved in a criminal lifestyle, involved in drug-dealing, or in underage alcohol abuse, or engaged in under-age sexual activity, your self-esteem is gathered from these areas, and not gathered from academic achievement," he argues.

An academic school simply trying to push disengaged young people through a regimented educational programme was lowering their self-esteem.

> "What we had to do was address their self-image. This was where I became very interested in behavioural management: you had to step into their world, to adjust their view. It is very difficult when dealing drugs is delivering a much higher income than perhaps training to become a joiner or a car mechanic. There is no incentive to delay gratification," he says.

A legitimate response from young Scots was why would you waste your time in 'loser professions', which might mean working in a café, a restaurant, a call centre or a care home, when you could make more money dealing in drugs or breaking into houses.

> "They see 'successful' drug dealers driving around in blacked-out Range Rovers. The dealer might die before he is 40, but what

conception does a 13-year-old have about this?" he says.

Graham began deploying his theories in a practical way with young people at Govan, refining them at Newlands Junior College.

"It is never a done deal. What we did was training throughout the year and based on my very early models. What informs these models is the current student body and what they are thinking and having to deal with outside the place of learning," he says.

In recent years, the dominance of social media has become an extra factor. Smart phones and the stream of content that is consumed by young, often impressionable, people can have a disproportionate influence on behaviour and wellbeing unless there are clear guidelines.

"Schools are very good at banning things, rather than adapting. When a teacher sees an opportunity to educate, they should be grabbing it, not banning something," he says.

There was growing appreciation that perceptual or cognitive impairment, such as dyslexia, learning disabilities and emotional and behavioural difficulties (EBD), made life more difficult for many young people. Often such impairments went undetected in mainstream secondary schools resulting in a lack of skills, poor levels of motivation and wilful indiscipline. In 1999, a study of young offenders in Scottish institutions found over a third could be identified as having previously undiagnosed dyslexia.

At Newlands, Graham was determined to understand every individual's capabilities and build on the self-images of young people under his charge.

Gillian Hunt captured one case study which exemplified this work.[52] Lucy [not her real name] was able to build a new self-image for herself. She was looked after and accommodated by Glasgow City Council, who acted as her corporate parent. When Lucy was a student at Newlands Junior College she was living with foster carers. When a child is in foster care, that living situation is known as a placement, not simply as her home. During her time at Newlands her placement failed, which meant she could no longer live with those carers and new foster carers and a new home had to be found.

Lucy's school experience was fractured as she lived in unsettling conditions.

She is dyslexic and has what she describes as "heavy, bad anxiety". Primary school had been fine but secondary school was completely different.

52 Ibid: Gillian Hunt, 2020.

She struggled at mainstream secondary school and felt she got little help. She would often end up in class sitting doing nothing. She failed her exams and was made to feel that it was all her fault. She was made to feel stupid.

"Teachers need to have patience. I had to do French for two years, and I just didn't get it. If you ask for help, you get into trouble and then you get made to stand outside. Compared to in primary if you ask somebody for help, the teacher goes, 'What's wrong?' And like the teacher helps you. You don't get that in high school," she explained to Gillian Hunt.

How was this different when she moved to Newlands?

"If you're struggling with something they actually help you ... if there's a change in your behaviour, they actually do something to help you...they actually care about your future," said Lucy.

The junior college student believes that if she had not attended Newlands, she would have spent a whole year not in school and doing nothing. She knew she lacked confidence in her abilities and needed teachers to assure her that she did, indeed, have potential.

When Newlands closed Lucy had only attended for one year and still had a year of school to go as she was not yet 16. She sat and passed exams in the year that she was at Newlands, "I sat all my Nat 4's. I could have sat my Nat 5's, I did have the potential, but I ran out of time."

Her view is that class sizes in secondary schools are too big and she recognises how difficult it is for teachers to provide individual help and support. In her school her pastoral care teacher had all the pupils whose surnames began with A to K, and that was 300 students. She felt that they did not have the time to deal with any student difficulties. Lucy believes that we need to make changes in schools because "it just doesn't work".

At the time of writing, Lucy is a 17-year-old, classed as a care leaver and living in supported accommodation. For Lucy, this means staying with a single woman who provides a room and meals within her home. This person has no responsibility for Lucy, other than providing a safe place for her to live and being on hand should Lucy need advice.

"Lucy needs so much more than this. She needs a consistent, strong network of support around her. Newlands Junior College is still providing some of this support, mainly from Elizabeth Orenes who was her mentor while she was a student there," says Gillian Hunt.

Even after the junior college's closure, Orenes continued to mentor and support Lucy in a number of significant ways: she supported her into this accommodation; met her on a weekly and sometimes daily basis; took her on outings and she supported her in both care and education meetings. Elizabeth Orenes was one of the trusted adult that Lucy relied upon. Planning and securing longer term care and support remains challenging for Lucy.

In several interviews with Gillian Hunt, parents and carers explained how "almost overnight" there were dramatic changes in the children who were now part of the Newlands Junior College 'family'. Claire McKay, the mother of Michael, said:

> "Newlands Junior College is the best thing that's ever happened to him ... he's a totally different boy, happier, thinking about his apprenticeship, mature, more confident ... all this has been noticed by grandparents and friends ... school does not seem to be able to bend for children ... NJC planted the seed and gave him the tools to progress." [53]

Another mother, Hazel Rutherford, could not believe the difference in her daughter Natalie [54], who had dyslexia and found that the mainstream school was not dealing with it well enough. She would do anything to get out of class, though she wasn't cheeky. Hazel felt that teachers did not look into the reasons for her behaviour. The school recommended Newlands to Natalie's parents. When Hazel found out about Newlands, she felt that it "ticked all the boxes" for her daughter's needs. When asked if there was anything she would change about NJC she said nothing, just have more of them (colleges).

> "The difference in Natalie unbelievable, she has confidence, belief in herself: she can't believe she can do what she's doing now ... NJC has given her confidence, it has shown her she can do it".

Sir Harry Burns, the former Scottish Government's Chief Medical Officer, writing in support of funding for Newlands in March 2017, [55] said:

> "Many young people see school as a waste of time. They feel they have no prospects and are unlikely to succeed in any career. Why should they try at school? Entry to Newlands Junior College tells them they have a future and the support of adults they learn to trust and respect gives them a sense of agency ... if we are to narrow the attainment gap in Scottish schools, more attention needs to be paid to the social

---

53 Ibid, Gillian Hunt, 2020.
54 Ibid, Gillian Hunt, 2020.
55 Letter to Scottish Government in support of Promoting and Funding Junior Colleges, 9 March 2017.

context of the pupils as a determinant of success. The model in use at Newlands Junior College clearly does this."

This was ringing endorsement from a highly respected Scottish scientist and public figure.

CHAPTER FOURTEEN:
College Days: The Early Years of Progress

News of the junior college sparked a great deal of external interest. Henry Hepburn, a journalist with the *TES Scotland*, reported on his visit in April 2015, six months after the opening when there were 23 students, mostly boys, with another 30 due to arrive in the summer.

All of the students were smartly turned out in black trousers, and optional skirt for the girls, white shirt and white, red and grey school ties, or in the embossed 'NJC' red school sweatshirt. It was normal for the staff to be wearing suits with a shirt and the school tie too.

> "A school given over to vocational education should be noisy, right? Lots of hammering and hollering, a perpetual clatter and chatter of hands-on endeavour. Newlands Junior College in Glasgow confounds that notion: in this controversial venture, designed to give a second chance to teens who were getting lost in the school system, a sense of calm prevails," said his report.[56]

The reporter described the ambience as more like an airline's executive lounge rather than a 'harum-scarum school' corridor.

> "Visitors are greeted by sleek furniture and bold colours. A row of bar stools and iMacs sits among floor-to-ceiling painted silhouettes of billowing trees. Students and staff wander casually, perusing their phones and supping coffees or energy drinks."

If the reporter witnessed the students sipping sugary 'energy drinks' it was short lived because the food and snacks prepared by Mary Rossi and Caroline Turnbull were designed to be as healthy as possible for the students.

Hepburn's report mentioned McColl as a Glaswegian billionaire who made his fortune in the engineering industry.

> "He has few qualms about venturing into controversial territory, having backed the Yes campaign in the independence referendum and attempts

---

56 Times Educational Supplement Scotland (TESS), April 2015.

to revive Rangers Football Club after its liquidation in 2012. But in a country with a strong tradition of state-run education, and a city that is the spiritual home of British socialism, this may be an even bolder venture," he wrote.

It summed up the challenge facing McColl and the junior college. Hepburn's report was warm and encouraging with positive comments from the students. Keeley Marshall, 14, said he was treated like an adult and that he worked better because there were fewer people in the class, while Edward Pert, also 14, said the staff spoke to him with respect, and that you could have a laugh with them.

"Students see little sense of hierarchy — they can call staff by their first names — and they like it that no teacher shouts," said the report. "Newlands promises every student that after two years they will be guaranteed an apprenticeship or a place on a college course. Dylan McCafferty, 14, says this guarantee motivates students: 'You're more confident — you're not thinking if you fail you're not going to get anywhere'."

.....

How was the college actually doing in those early months? The first inspection from HM Inspectors, in September 2015, when there were 48 students in the junior college, was extremely positive and captured the essence of the college in its opening year.

"Young people are enthusiastic about their learning. They describe how staff use the modern and well-resourced learning environment to engage them in their lessons and encourage their participation," said inspector Lesley Johnstone. [57]

The inspector found a positive attitude to learning which was demonstrated by almost all young people. There was a welcoming ethos, supportive relationships between all adults and the young people, and a range of partners delivering interesting learning experiences in an attractive, modern and well-resourced environment for learning. [58]

---

57 Education Scotland, Inspectors' Report, 27 October 2015
58 Ibid, 27 October 2015.

"Young people who spoke to inspectors described how the helpful approaches taken by all staff at Newlands Junior College have encouraged them to learn effectively and re-engage in their studies. They particularly appreciate having positive and supportive relationships with teachers. Young people say they are enjoying learning practical skills alongside theory. They like the choice of vocational topics, such as construction, hairdressing and engineering for which they attend City of Glasgow College. Young people also enjoy attending the Riverside Music Complex to study music technology. The junior college has developed productive partnerships with a range of organisations and groups to enhance learners' experiences," said the inspection report, which noted the key partners were Glasgow Training Group (GTG) and Skill Force.

Jim Biggin, closely involved with the Work Experience Programme, said one of his personal highs in 2016 and 2017 was that *"Almost without exception, our students have stepped up to the mark, and have proved to potential employers, that they are 'work ready' and we have had some excellent reports on their performances."*

Jim McColl was also in the public eye for the rescue of Ferguson's shipyard in Port Glasgow on the Clyde. This was the totemic place because it was the last commercial shipyard on the Clyde, and McColl was asked by the then First Minister Alex Salmond to intervene to save the yard. He did this in the autumn of 2014, and while there was initial success and substantial investment, the yard became embroiled in a bitter dispute involving CMAL, the Scottish Government's arm-length owner of Scotland's ferries and harbour facilities, who were ordering new vessels. In the honeymoon period after McColl took over the yard, a group of junior college students were given stimulating work experience at the yard, and a number were given Modern Apprenticeships at Ferguson Marine.

Meantime, White and his colleagues were still learning how to enhance the junior college culture and a Rapid Approach to School Self-Evaluation was adopted and viewed as successful. This would be the template for future inspections.

"Overall, the junior college's approaches to self-evaluation and improvement planning are at an early stage of development.

The Principal and promoted staff have themselves identified the need to now implement robust approaches to evaluating their work, so that improvement can be well planned and put in place to further support young people's life chances," said the inspectors' report.

According to the inspectors, these were important areas of improvement for the Principal and the college trustees to consider, which would ensure the wellbeing of young people, tracking their progress across their learning and continuing to challenge and support them.

Keir Bloomer and Douglas Clark set about developing a skills taxonomy to log individual students' development which covered communication skills, numeracy and employability. In 2017, two further areas of IT and cognitive skills were added.

"At present, there is an orthodoxy in Scottish education that nothing influences the quality of provision other than the quality of teaching. That is not true. There are lots of other factors, such as the curriculum and the nature of education policy, that influence the way in which the system is performing and, therefore, the experience of the individual," said Bloomer. [59]

English teacher Victoria Rose, who took over from Samantha Wrigglesworth, was given the task of raising the literacy level of the student population. *"All students will be involved in semi-structured interviews before the end of February 2017 to ascertain their own perception of literacy and their mastery of appropriate skills."* [60]

Each student was to be regularly tested and given a Skill Log to act as a literacy journal tracking progress across subjects with Newlands. This really mattered to the teaching staff.

By 2017, Rose was regularly highlighting the challenges many had with very low reading ages. This was a continuing concern, seriously hindering young people's development and urgent action was required. Students were assessed using the STAR Reading Test. In 2017, 61% of Year One had a reading age of nine or less. By the end of 2018, only 29% were in this category, with another 29% above the reading age of 11.

59 Scottish Parliament, Education and Skills Committee, 23 January 2019, Keir Bloomer evidence.
60 NJC Progress Report, Number 9, March 2017.

"In Year Two, the percentage of students significantly or worryingly below the benchmark has fallen from 45% to 35% over their time with us; the percentage who are slightly below, below or worryingly below the benchmark has fallen from 45% to 33%." [61]

Bloomer became aware of a discrepancy between academic and employment expectation which also needed fixing. Newlands, Arnold Clark and GTG Training developed a recruitment process which was better able to measure maths, arithmetic, English and basic sciences competency and tailored for those seeking Modern Apprenticeships in the motor trade.

Philip Graham and Suzanne Sherry, head of apprenticeships at Arnold Clark, opened up frank discussions, and Victoria Rose and Douglas Clark began to revamp their basic courses to bring it into closer alignment with the SQA National Certificate and the GTG Training test.

"We found that people might have a pass at Nat 4 and Nat 5, but when it came to our skills test there was a discrepancy. For example, working out fractions was not properly understood. We found that some people applying to us did not have a basic understanding. We shared our skills test with Newlands and explained what we were looking for. They were able to take the base of the SQA tests and enhance it, so that when young people came to us, they were passing the skills test first time," says Eddie Hawthorne.

This was not purely a Newlands initiative for Arnold Clark, but it was one where Rose and Clark were at the forefront.

Why was this so important for Eddie Hawthorne?

"We, the business people, were bringing the business acumen and the ability to provide employment for the young people, but the teaching staff brought their undoubted skills and outstanding commitment. Victoria and Douglas were very talented teachers who were engaging with the young people. In my opinion, these relationships were what made the college. It was like a small family," says Hawthorne.

The author's interview with Eddie Hawthorne was undertaken in the weeks before the COVID-19 pandemic changed the world through a lockdown, with a drastic impact on the transport industry, including public transport, aviation and car manufacturing. However, much of what Hawthorne stated about young people and employment remains relevant for a post COVID-19 economic recovery.

---

61 Newlands Junior College, Standards & Quality Report 2017-2018.

"I can speak for the car industry and it is changing really quickly. While we still need bricklayers, welders and car mechanics, we need IT people as well. My view of education is that I use the end product that they produce. If that end product is not good enough, I have to go somewhere else or invest our own time to make it better. We are talking about young people," he says. "By engaging employers at an earlier point in the education cycle, then children and young people will understand what is required of them and also employers can have an input into what society really needs in terms of employment," says Hawthorne.

All this raised the wider philosophical question: why do we educate young people if it is not to find a place of productive work. *"A large part of people's contribution to society is working and being able to add a value to your local community,"* he adds.

Practical science, applicable to the contemporary work environment, was always at the forefront. Kenny McDonald's science room and lab was buzzing as students breezed in and then out. The notes on the whiteboard during the author's visit instructed them what to do.

- Get your folder.

- Check the last activity you did.

- Prepare for the next activity and let Kenny know you're ready to do it. Then there was a reminder: "Have you updated your skills log?"

In Lab Science communications skills, the note was about using information. Finding out about the Health & Safety at Work Act, electrical safety and COSHH [the Control of Substances Hazardous to Health Regulations], and how to write a risk assessment, making notes on how to store dangerous chemicals. A risk assessment on storing dangerous chemicals? Quite a subject for students who less than a year earlier were disengaged from learning.

But the teaching staff needed to keep raising their game too. The General Teaching Council for Scotland was implementing a new system of Professional Update for teachers, signed off by head teachers or principals. Every teacher in Scotland was required to make a submission to the teaching council and Newlands' presentations to the Professional Update Endorsement Panel was sent on 15th December 2015. In early 2016, the teaching staff learned that its arrangements had been validated and accepted. Indeed, the panel commended the work being undertaken in relation to Professional Update and the engagement with staff. It stated the staff showed "*a clear commitment to collegiate and collaborative approaches in and beyond the college with a resolution focused approach to appeals processes.*"

.....

Trustee Scott Black spent a day at the college with the first cohort. They had already settled in and were doing well. Black was fired up by what he found.

> "My wife even said when I came back from the college, 'What happened to you today?' She thought it was the most energised I had come in to our house for donkey's years. And she didn't even know I was at the college," he says.

He came springing into the house full of chat about the exceptional young people he had met and the privilege of being involved.

> "I felt as if I had met a whole range of guys and girls who reminded me so much of my younger self. More than this, it reminded me of the kids that had been in my class at Govan. They were almost Identikits. There was a mixture of quiet people, loud people, daft people, gregarious folk and gallus young guys."

While some still had their problems, the students were engaged and chatting.

> "Someone accused us of cherry-picking children, that we had just picked a bundle of bright kids. Obviously, they were bright kids but they were all falling out of school when we got them. All the junior college did was just turn them round."

At one early trustees' meeting, Black asked: "What would you have as an acceptable failure rate for the college?" Jim McColl intervened and asked him to rephrase this because he preferred not to use the term "failure" when referring to young people.

> "OK, what do you regard as the success rate, then. Is it 90%."

It was a good example of how McColl invited people to adopt a more positive mindset. In Black's view, landing a third of the cohort onto the right path for a positive destination would seem a remarkable story. In reality, it would be substantially more than this.

An essential part of reaching a positive mindset for the students was the involvement of Skill Force Scotland, a third-sector organisation which recruited ex-armed forces personnel. In the college's first year, the achievements were outstanding with all but three attaining ASDAN Bronze, and Duke of Edinburgh and Outward Bound Trust certificates. The college was fortunate to have two charismatic instructors in Billy Huxter and then Phil Carr, both former military men who must be acknowledged for their work in developing the students.

Huxter joined the team in July 2014 and took the first cohort of students to the Blane Valley in June 2015 to complete their Duke of Edinburgh expedition. Billy had served for 22 years in the British Army, latterly as a quartermaster and motor transport manager. When he left the Army in 2007 he became a Skill Force instructor. Under his guidance, the college was awarded a certificate for the 'Most Innovation in Skill, Physical or Volunteering Section of the Year, in Glasgow's Education Services awards. The certificate for the 2015 group was signed and presented by Maureen McKenna.

Rugby union and association football were a big part of the fun for many of the males, with several Glasgow Warriors professional rugby players coming to the college to speak about their motivation and training. A nascent rugby squad began at Newlands but Scotland's national sport, football, still had a stranglehold. In June 2016, Skillvalley played against Dukla Pumpherson, at the Excelsior Stadium, home of Airdrie FC. Five Newlands students turned-out, Connor, Jamie, Robbie, Paul and Giancarlo, as well as Dougie and Billy Huxter. "*The game was against a very good team of ex-professionals who have a great record of participating in charity matches. As expected, our students were excellent and even helped with goals. Sadly we lost 6-5, however the experience was one which was thoroughly enjoyed by all. A special thank you goes out to Kevin Lynch, Skill Force for allowing us this great opportunity to be involved in the charity event,*" posted Billy Huxter on Facebook.

Billy and Phil Carr along with Graham Robertson took the cohort to Loch Eil on one of the trips, spending the weekend in the Outward Bound Trust dormitories, in Achdalieu, near Fort William. Out on a hill walk, the boys discovered a frog, trapped it in a plastic bag and decided to take the amphibian back to Glasgow. They fed it blades of grass and hid it in their belongings in the dorm. The instructors became concerned about the furtive behaviour. They even thought there might be drug misuse involved until they discovered the boys were caring for the frog. There was great relief and hilarity from the teaching stuff.

Phil Carr took over from Billy in September 2016. Carr, originally from

Kingston-upon-Hull, left his home city and joined the Royal Navy in HMS Ganges in November 1973. He entered as a Junior Naval Airman (Aircraft Handler) and trained to work on aircraft carrier flight decks in aircraft operations, crash rescue and air traffic control. He served on two different Ark Royal aircraft carriers, the second as the Flight Deck Captain in charge of all flight deck operations.

"During active service I was involved in operational tours in the Arabian Gulf twice, Hong Kong during the Boat People crisis, and in NATO operations in Bosnia and in Northern Ireland. Towards the end of my active service I became the Chief Instructor at the School of Flight Deck operations for two years," he said.

He spent some time within the Ministry of Defence and in 1996 he transferred to the Naval Careers Service and retrained as a careers advisor spending six years working in Edinburgh, Glasgow and Hull. He joined Skill Force in 2002 and was working as an instructor in various schools before joining Newlands, where he delivered employability sessions to both year groups.

Skill Force would became an essential element in Newlands' success story. On Monday 30th April 2018, the new Prince William Award, a pre-Duke of Edinburgh Award for young people, was formally launched in the House of Lords and Phil Carr was asked to take part in the formal presentation to around 200 guests. The impact of the Prince William Award across schools has been 'profound' he told the audience.

"My part in the presentation was being asked to give a brief insight into my early life, my service in the Royal Navy, the Royal Navy Careers Service and my time with Skill Force. As part of the talk I discussed the variety of roles I have undertaken with Skill Force in different local authorities. I also spoke about my present duties at Newlands Junior College and my role and my experiences delivering the Prince William award on a Friday morning in Kilmarnock." [62]

There were countless moments of mirth and amusement on the day trips and outward bound excursions. On a walk to Muirshiel Country Park and Duchal Moor in 2017, with Phil and Douglas, two of the girls found a sluice gate on a reservoir with railings and re-enacted a scene from the *Titanic* film.

---

62 NJC, Progress Report, No 14, June 2018.

CHAPTER FIFTEEN:
A View from a Non-Teaching Insider: The NJC Mother

One woman who became ingrained with college life and the welfare of its students was Elizabeth Orenes. She stepped in to become the office manager in October 2016 and discovered a surprising new vocation in life as the 'NJC Mother!'

Since 2002, she had been employed by Clyde Blowers, working as the personal assistant to Bill Thomson, a trained engineer who was the innovative partner of Jim McColl for over 20 years as they built their successful international company. Thomson had spent a lot of time in China where he negotiated several deals for the East Kilbride business, and opened up major opportunities, and he later became the managing director of InterBulk, a logistics firm which was owned by Clyde Blowers. He was from a working-class family in Dumbarton, and his father was a butcher, and he shared McColl's views on the importance of education and its application to the work place. Thomson had prospered as one of McColl's closest colleagues. Elizabeth Orenes had enjoyed working for Thomson, but when he stepped back from his work with Clyde Blowers, her job was no longer necessary.

> "I was asked if I could give a bit of professional assistance at Newlands on the accounting side of things. I came in to process the invoices and that's when I stepped up to do the expenses and the pay roll for salaries," says Orenes. [63]

While the college paid no VAT as a registered Scottish charity, its wages and salaries for the eight staff, six of whom were academic, were around £343,000 a year, with social security costs of around £30,000 and pension contributions of around £60,000. The existing office manager Lesley Mackenzie, who had been at the college since its inception, was heading off on maternity leave. Lesley became unwell at this time and had to leave her work without time for a proper hand-over. Elizabeth's new role grew rapidly.

> "I had never worked in a school before in my life. I just got thrown into the deep end. I didn't know anything about the SQA. And I wasn't

---

63 Elizabeth Orenes interview with the author, July 2019.

used to dealing with a lot of young people from the 14 to 16-age-group," she adds.

Lesley Mackenzie was popular with the students and Orenes felt naturally there might have been resentment by some who assumed she had taken over Lesley's job, so her first challenge was establishing her own position. As she puts it, the madness ensued but it was an incredibly rewarding journey. It would take 20 minutes by car from her home in East Kilbride to the college, arriving for 8.30am. In these first few days she dreaded coming down to the college. There was a suggestion that perhaps coming from the Clyde Blowers' head office, information might be filtered back to McColl. But that was never the case. Orenes was loyal and supportive to the college and its aims. *"By Christmas time, I was running to work. I just loved it and I knew that we were making a great difference to some young lives,"* she says.

Despite having a young family, her children were then aged 11, 5, and 2, she often ended up working late on week nights to help with the students' demands. She is highly organised and methodical, and had a lot more to offer than processing the invoices and expenses and very soon she became immersed in all the non-teaching activities of the junior college. The third and fourth intakes of students arrived during her time at Newlands.

"I became heavily involved in the general administration, and the recruitment process along with Douglas Clark. So I went out to meet the schools with Douglas where we were able to speak about the benefits of the college, and prepare people for their arrival at Newlands," she says.

Scott Black recalls that the issue of recruitment was permanently on the board agenda at trustee meetings.

"We would talk long and hard about how to convey the message to secondary school teachers about why they should nominate students to us. As trustees, we were all learning. Apart from Keir, we really did not have the educational experience. We had our views based on personal experience, but we now needed to understand the drivers for a secondary school head teacher. Why wouldn't every secondary school in the Glasgow area, nominate a couple of children to us?" he says. [64]

---

64 Scott Black interview with the author, September 2019.

For Black, it seemed an obvious decision for schools where there were young people regularly dodging classes. Clark and Orenes were dispatched to Glasgow schools already nominating candidates.

> "We were able to explain who we were and what we were looking for at the junior college. In many instances, the pastoral care staff in the schools was changing, so we needed to keep up with the new contacts," says Orenes.

After this out-reach, the interested school staff were invited to an information evening at Newlands where further questions would be answered by White and Graham.

There were only nine secondary schools during the five-year history of Newlands willing to make a connection. The rest, where there might well have been suitable candidates, snubbed the junior college, including Govan High after White and Graham departed.

> "That was very disappointing. There were schools that were not engaged with what we were trying to do. However, from the schools that we were involved with, the nominations became stronger and better, and in the latter years we got a more suitable type of intake," says Orenes.

How did students respond to their arrival at Newlands?

> "Of course, it depended on the individuals because all of the intakes were quite different. For most of them, it was about building their confidence. They had been told for so long that they were not very good, that they started to believe this."

Once they realised life at Newlands was very different from their mainstream school experience, they responded positively. Several students' parents were in such a dysfunctional state that they did not get up in the morning to ensure their child had a proper breakfast, or lunch money and bus fares to go to school. A Newlands scholarship provided a full package of day-time care and extra-curricular activities as well as an education. "*It was clear then that the young people started to trust you,*" says Orenes.

Speaking at a Reform Scotland [65] conference on education in January 2021, Alex Stewart explained: "*In the first six weeks of each year, I would say*

---

65 Reform Scotland's Commission on School Reform: "Engaging the Disengaged – Alternative Approaches to Education", 21 January 2021.

'Gosh, we've been lucky in the previous year, previous two years, previous three at Newlands. Now we've got a bunch of rowdy kids who are going to rip this place up'. Yet it was always transformational how, when that relationship came to be real, the young people and the adults believed in each other and moved forward together."

Orenes recalls one un-named 14-year-old girl from an early cohort who lived in foster care. The girl sat for the first few days in one of the booths with her head down and would not look at anyone. She didn't move during her break-time.

It was baby steps with the staff asking; "*How's your day been?*" or "*How are you feeling about things?*" That was normally enough for the first engagement. Then after a few more days: "*What have you enjoyed at college today?*" It was all about building a level of trust. Slowly and gently, she began to get involved in the wider activity and socialisation of the college.

"Now we have a really good relationship based on trust," says Orenes.

Orenes said the student personalities were all so different. Another girl was very loud and 'in-your-face'. This presented itself as an aggressive personality, when in truth, it was an out-going young woman who had never been properly encouraged or shown direction. With patience and calmness from the staff, she learned to modify her behaviour without losing her natural personality, which became essential for her work choice. She has now gone on to become a hairdresser and still keeps in contact.

Over the months, Orenes earned a new moniker, when she was dubbed 'The NJC Mum', a badge which she wore with pride. She received numerous thank you cards from students referring to her as their 'NJC Mum'.

"I loved it. I'm old enough to be their Mum. It didn't affect me in the slightest. They can come and speak to me about anything and I loved that part of the job."

Orenes was privy to personal details, disclosed with trust, which had not even been shared with their own mothers. Much of this was to do with puberty, relationships, sexual activity and how to handle new and awkward emotional situations. For the girls, it was easier for them to speak with another female than perhaps taking the matter to a male head teacher. Philip Graham, as Child Protection Officer, worked hand in glove with Orenes on looking out for the students.

"The students were brilliant. I felt a strong sense of pride just like a mother. When I saw them on graduation day, I was beaming with delight for them all. Seeing how far they had come on their journey was amazing. I don't know how I wasn't crying my eyes out," she says.

When the students were picked up at 2.30pm for their lifts home, Elizabeth Orenes reverted to her original role as the office manager. While this involved the invoices and expenses, after the departure of Jim Biggin, the maintenance and facilities person, who also doubled as a driver and chief exam invigilator, she took up this position too. One of the major recurring costs were further education fees and transport. The fees due to City of Glasgow College for the vocational courses were substantial, running at over £100,000 a year, and paid at a commercial rate. From 9am until 12 noon, students were taken by minibus out to the City of Glasgow in Cathedral Street or Thistle Street for various courses.

The timetable on the office wall was clear:

Monday AM	NPA Administration Activities (Joint Y1 & Y2 Class); Sport (Joint Y1 & Y2 Class); and Maritime Operations (Y2 Class)
Monday PM	Engineering (Y1 Class) and Construction (Y2 Class)
Tuesday AM	Food & Hospitality
Tuesday PM	Hairdressing (Y1 Class) and Food & Hospitality (Y2 Class)
Wednesday AM	Construction (Y2 Class)
Thursday PM	Hairdressing (Y2 Class)
Friday PM	Early Education and Childcare (Joint Y1 & Y2 Class); Construction Y1 Class and Engineering Y2.

When the college began there was a single minibus and a number of taxis. As the intake increased, they needed a second minibus, with Arnold Clark stepping in to supply a new vehicle.

"The junior college was not a school. It did not look like a school, feel like a school or operate like a school. This was crucial to those disengaged young people who had switched off from school and from learning. Health and wellbeing were also important. In order to mitigate the effects of poverty (70% of the cohort who came from the most disadvantaged areas) young people were collected by minibuses in the morning and brought into the college for breakfast. A healthy lunch and snacks were also provided. Students were transported to vocational courses and work experience placements and back home at the end of the day," [66] says Gillian Hunt.

[66] Ibid, Gillian Hunt, 2020.

CHAPTER SIXTEEN:

Red and White Ties: Pride in the Badge

Hampden Park, Scotland's National football stadium, was a 15-minute walk from Newlands Junior College in Inverlair Avenue, so it was the ideal setting for the First Graduation Ceremony on Wednesday, 22nd June 2016.

> "This was a red letter day for the junior college. It was the first time that our students had completed two years with us and they were ready to move on. It was a very special moment for students, parents and carers. A day that I will never, ever, forget," says White.

The invitation was extended for a buffet lunch before the graduation ceremony at 2pm with brief speeches from Jim McColl and Iain White.

Everyone had made an effort to look their best and every one of the students proudly wore their red, white and grey school ties with crisp white shirts. Dress code was an important part of the daily life of the college and, for graduation, were reminded that all required to wear plain, black school trousers and skirt. *Jogging trousers were not acceptable.* 19 young people graduated on the day and all were heading on to positive destinations, eight into employment, six continuing with a Foundation engineering programme at City of Glasgow College, and a further five undertaking National Certificate courses at City of Glasgow College.

> "We are here at this very special location to mark an equally special occasion as our first group of students graduate and head through the doorway that leads to the rest of their lives," McColl told the gathering.

> "The way it was pitched as a Junior College was very important. The students were proud of the whole place. It wasn't a 'special school' where you were packed off to because you were a trouble-maker. It was a Junior College which offered you a different path," said McColl.

The graduations were a personal and emotional experience for Eddie Hawthorne.

> "That first graduation was a real high point for me. The celebration of the very first cohort was special because these young people had never really experienced success before. To see the delight in their faces when they actually did have success, which was shared with their parents or

carers, was genuinely humbling. Witnessing this success was what kept a lot of us involved," says the motor industry boss.[67]

The 19 students exceeded what was predicted for them at the time of their enrolment. The following passes were:

	National 3	National 4	National 5
English	2	17	4
IT		19	
Maths	1	18	
Physics	3	16	
Laboratory Science			19
Total	**6**	**70**	**23**

More than this, seven achieved the ASDAN Gold Award and all but one succeeded at either Bronze of Silver, and, among other certificates, 95% were awarded the SQA Employability Certificate. This was an exceptional record, which Newlands said was "*possibly unprecedented in Scotland*". [68]

The inspectors were clearly impressed too when they said: "*Almost all young people have shown resilience and responsibility to gain a range of personal achievement awards.*"

Furthermore, in the funding letter in March 2017 to the Scottish Government, there was more encouraging news.

> "There are strong indications that the performance of the second cohort will surpass that of the first. For example, two students passed National 5 English at the end of their first year and numerous students have passed most or all of their assessments at National 4 in all of the subjects on offer. Two students have been verified as having passed all of the units for Higher English and one is likely to sit the exam with a good chance of obtaining the qualification in S4." [69]

This was quite an achievement in less than two years in operation. The Newlands' staff and the trustees began to consider what could be achieved with more time and a secure, long-term future.

Graduation was certainly not seen as the end by Newlands. The staff made

67 Eddie Hawthorne interview with the author, February 2020.
68 Proposal from Newlands Junior College to Scottish Government: Promoting and funding junior colleges, 24 March 2017.
69 Ibid. 24 March 2017.

sustained efforts to stay in touch with all former students and to help them in whatever way might be needed.

Graham Robertson's job as principal teacher of guidance involved helping young people into positive destinations. As it developed, he saw his role as having a much longer-term outlook. Getting young people into full-time jobs, Foundation and Modern Apprenticeships, or FE college courses was very worthwhile but often only half the story. Many students needed extra support to stay there. Robertson spent a great deal of time helping former students to stick with their 'positive destinations'. Sometimes, he helped them to move to new opportunities. The junior college did not give up on its alumni.

CHAPTER SEVENTEEN:
Outsiders Looking In:
The College Wins Local Support

Local associate minister Wilma Pearson was doing the rounds of her parishioners in the Cathcart community. She noticed a group of students entering the college. Her curiosity kicked in and she went in to introduce herself.

> "I wanted to know more about the college and why they were there because, as locals, we hadn't heard very much about the opening. I was trying to find out what it was about," she recalls. [70]

Iain White was delighted to meet her and showed her around.

> "He explained the ethos of the school, which I immediately bought into. I have seen too many youngsters who have fallen by the wayside. I thought it was really exciting what they were doing."

Her question was: *how can I help?* The college was not looking for a school chaplain, although she already undertook this role at another Glasgow educational establishment. She was encouraged to be a 'friend' of the junior college and just drop in any time. White said it was about connecting with the young people.

> "This daunted me a wee bit at first because it was very unstructured. I did it though. Some of the students weren't interested in conversation. That was fine, but it soon began to change," she says.

This was not a religious role but she assured people that the local church, which she represented, cared and had indeed prayed for its success.

> "I reckon the role that fitted best for me was to be there as a listener and to be there for the staff. At the end it was a matter of listening to the grieving process of the staff when the college was closing, appreciating they were losing something special that they had created."

The relationship built up and the church facilities were used for college examinations. The reciprocal use was the college was used by the church

70 The Rev. Wilma Pearson interview with the author, 23 September 2019.

for one of its elders' conferences on a Saturday. This was a true sense of the college and the local church being part of the community. Wilma Pearson had been a primary teacher before her calling to serve God and she had some insight into learning and teaching.

.....

A magical snapshot of Newlands Junior College was the coffee mornings, hosted by the students and supported by church goers and others in the local community. Wilma Pearson watched with astonishment at the young people's development and growing maturity.

The college had opened in a quiet residential street in the south side of Glasgow and was not well known. A joint initiative by students and staff was needed and a funding committee, including Scott Black and Alex Stewart, advised the students. It was all part of the involvement of the students, and made them appreciate, in a small way, that it was not simply a 'take' relationship, but that they were expected to give something back, however small that might be. The junior college's funding was explained at a workshop looking at how to increase involvement. The students started to come up with their own ideas. "*Would it help if we washed the vehicles,*" suggested one student. This raised the issue of why would they wash the vehicles. There was discussion about saving money on cleaning and how to let outsiders in the local community know about the pride students felt for their junior college. This developed with students suggesting they undertake car washing and valeting. Perhaps this wasn't really what the junior college staff had in mind, considering the reputation of dubious car washing businesses in Glasgow, so the conversation was moved up in tone.

"Why don't we run a coffee morning and invite people in to meet us from the local community," suggested another.

"Why do you want to do this? " asked Black.

"Because they all think we're thick-heads who turn up at school here. We want to show them we are not," said another.

So the idea of a coffee morning was born. The students made up the flyers — Happiness is a Cup of Coffee —and even wrote letters to some local influencers, such as a church and youth club leaders, to explain what was going on at the college. These flyers were taken out and put up in local shops and it raised the awareness of the coffee morning on Friday 15th December 2017 at 10.30am until noon.

128

Alongside the flyers were personal letters from some of the students:

Dear Neighbour of Newlands Junior College,

Our names are James and Liam and we are new students at Newlands Junior College. We are writing to let you know a bit about us. We were nominated to be part of the Newlands Junior College family by our pastoral care teachers at our old schools, as we weren't really liking school and got into some bother. But we have rapidly changed since joining Newlands Junior College.

….. The letter explained the college was planning some community events and concluded:

"At Newlands Junior College we can't wait to get to know the local area and hopefully you are looking forward to getting to know us. Please feel welcome to come in for a visit or get in contact to see what we are doing and find out more about us," Yours sincerely Liam and James.

The local response to the coffee morning was fantastic, according to Elizabeth Orenes, and Eures, a local catering company, supplied some wonderful chocolate brownies and other goodies. *"Everybody wanted to help in some way because they knew what we were trying to do,"* says Orenes.

It was about connecting with the community and with business people, and preparing the young students for the world of work.

"I was impressed with them," says Wilma Pearson. "They were proud of themselves and had a degree of self-confidence. They were polite and courteous. They were keen to help. Yes, it was good public relations, but it was also about people skills and how young people learn to behave and handle themselves. It was about being respectful of other people, all of this within the ethos of the junior college."

One guest commented on Facebook: *"Had a wonderful time. You should be very proud of your students. They were all so smart and polite, had a very informative and interesting tour, keep up the great work."*

The junior college replied: *"Coffee morning is a soaraway success! Thank you to all our friends – old and new for coming along and having a chat. It means so much to our students for the community to join with us."*

…..

The Rev. Pearson was invited to the Third Graduation Ceremony at the City of Glasgow College on Wednesday, 20th June 2018. There was a buffet lunch followed by the ceremony which began at 2pm. This was for the students who had joined in August 2016. All 13 graduates were heading on to positive destinations, seven into Modern Apprenticeships, five with National Certificate courses at the City of Glasgow College and Riverside Studios, and one returning to mainstream school to complete Secondary. This represented a 100% result of positive destinations.

> "It was heart-warming to be at the graduation and see the students. There were two things that touched me: one was the relationship between the staff and students, the fact that they were one and even wore the same junior college tie. It was an indication that, 'We are all in this together.' Even at the graduation there was a bit of good-hearted banter and backchat, which is not what you usually get at a school ceremony. This was because it was about relationships," says the Rev. Pearson.

She said the young people were being treated like adults and expected to be respectful, with an element of this respect being able to pull one another's leg.

> "As an observer, I loved seeing the proud parents and carers. That made me emotional because these young people were not making it in mainstream education and weren't expected to do well and their parents were seeing them succeed. As a parent, that was very important to me. Seeing these delighted grannies and, in many cases, the whole family all at the graduation supporting the young person."

She recalls meeting one young woman whom she had met before in other circumstances now flourishing at Newlands.

> "Seeing her blossom, gain confidence and become part of an educational establishment which encouraged her, brought me joy. I also know that it brought joy to the head teacher of her former school who was delighted that she had found an environment where she could flourish."

One young female student even offered to give Wilma a lesson in how to apply her make-up, eyeliner and eyelashes, which was greatly appreciated but gently declined.

The partnership with City of Glasgow College became a crucial one and during the graduation at the magnificent new campus facilities in Cathedral Street, City of Glasgow College's Depute Principal Sheila Lodge spoke warmly of the "very healthy" relationship which had evolved over the previous years.

Pearson is clear that the mainstream system should not be criticised because it was doing the best that it could do for the majority of young people, given the available resources.

> "I wouldn't want it to be called the 'sausage machine' but there are expectations on mainstream schools that they will achieve success rates and hit targets. Yet to support the very vulnerable, who are not doing well at school, you need far more staff and more resources. It's a political thing, but you need far more money to be put in, for one-to-one mentoring and the likes."

Pearson's sadness was that pupils in mainstream schools were slipping through the net.

> "I don't think it's deliberate but some young people give teachers such a hard time in school that the teachers are pleased when the troublesome people are off. Iain White said to me: 'If we can get their lives straight and get them stable and into employment, then they would be giving to society. If we didn't, then these would be the very young people who would end up in jail, and as addicts and end up with multiple children that were destined for care.' What role models would they be then? He said if the junior college could turn their lives around, then they would actually be a blessing. That was the word he used. They would be a blessing to society. This is what we want for everybody," she adds.

.....

There was another interlocking piece of the community jigsaw where the Rev. Pearson played her part. The Junior College required a driver to replace Jim Biggin and an inspired addition to the college was about to drive in. Donald Macleod was contemplatively seated in the pews at Cathcart Trinity church one Sunday morning when a notification flashed up on the Powerpoint screen in the pre-service intimations. "*Driver wanted. To help bring students to and from Newlands Junior College on weekday mornings from Monday to Friday.*"

It was a chilly February in 2016 and the retired Glasgow man from Outer Hebridean stock was unaware of this new institution in the district but thought he might be able to work with the youngsters. The Rev. Pearson was passing among her congregation and whispered to him: "*Did you see that advert for the driver? I think you would be brilliant for that.*" And that was the start. The following week, Donald was interviewed by Elizabeth Orenes and Philip Graham at the college and then met Iain White for final approval. "He was absolutely perfect. He was a former superintendent in the Glasgow police force, and he was the father of four daughters. You could feel the warmth from him," says Orenes.

> "My experience of life as a police officer and my love for my family seemed to matter, and what Iain, Elizabeth and Philip said to me really appealed. We should treat people with respect whoever they are, and if we can put an arm around their shoulder, then that's the way you should teach people," he says. [71]

Donald Macleod was keen to underplay the significance of his career, yet he joined the force in 1975, spending 31 years in the Strathclyde Police Force, and was a sergeant in Easterhouse and Cranhill, rising to become a superintendent. He had witnessed a great deal about the good and the bad of humanity throughout his time. While he spoke with a softer-Scottish accent and was polite and well-mannered, he knew how to deal with some of the toughest and most harrowing cases in the city.

> "I was very impressed with the junior college's ethos. When I was talking to Iain about how I had been seconded out of the police for a while on the Govan Initiative, we realised where we had met previously," he says.

Macleod called himself a 'driver/mentor'.

> "I'm not saying I got on well with all the kids. But I used to emphasise to them that I was *not* a teacher. I'm Donald Macleod and I was a retired police officer."

He found this was often the first positive contact the young people at Newlands had ever had with a police officer and, once they got to know him as a supportive individual, they would ask him about his service, often making jokes about his time.

> "They might say, 'You were in the polis!' I was not ashamed of that. I would say that it is a very good and important job. One or two of them even said they would like to 'join the polis'. I would reply,

---

71 Donald Macleod interview with the author, 23 September 2019.

'There's no reason why you shouldn't be. You have to stay out of bother and you have to show you are capable of doing it'. It was all very relevant to them. I loved the job. I loved the whole thing about building relationships with these young people," he says.

He was regularly asked about the crimes he was involved in — but his simple reply was:

"There isn't a crime you can mention that I wasn't involved in," he would say.

"Murders and a' that?" inquired one youngster.

"I'm not going to talk about it, but all I can say is there isn't a crime you can mention that I wasn't involved in over my 31 years."

The driver/mentor was a constant and consistent part of their Newlands Junior College experience.

The other driver was Chris Devlin, who was also a taxi driver, who arrived after the second 16-seater minibus was donated. With this transport facility in place, a proper pick-up and drop-off system was arranged for the students. This became their daily lifeline from home to their seat of learning.

With each new cohort, the logistics of home addresses and places to rendezvous were thrown into the discussion. Macleod would drive to the college from south-side home and pick up the minibus at 7am. He drove Bus Run No1 and he headed over to Knightswood for his first pick-ups, then back to Govan and Pollok. Bus Run No2, driven by Devlin, was more local trips around the south side, doing two runs to Gorbals, Cathkin, Nitshill and then out to Castlemilk.

"We encouraged them not to miss the minibus and then have to send a taxi for them. We tried to be quite firm on that," says Orenes.

The first pick-ups were at 7.30am, which was decidedly early for some students. A key factor was the arranged pick-up points were no more than ten minutes' walk from their homes or place of care. The students were expected to be waiting at the pick-up, although the drivers were prepared to wait perhaps two or three minutes before heading off. The use of Facebook was vital in letting students know that the 'red' or 'white' bus was caught in traffic, but on its way.

They [the drivers] would be there. It was all about the relationships. The students built up good relationships with both Donald and Chris, and did not want to let them down," says Orenes.

"Very rarely they let you down. There were one or two occasions when someone slept in, but not often. The young people were great," adds Macleod.

This was a vital backstop in ensuring attendance and a continuity of learning. If a student was not at the allocated pick-up point, there was a phone call to see what had happened, asking why they were not coming in and offering a taxi to bring them in, if there were special circumstances.

"I had one girl who was dropped off at her Grans and phoned to say she couldn't come in because she had no shoes. There were silly things like that when people were just 'at it'," says Orenes.

Just after 8am students started arriving at Inverlair Avenue and they would be given their breakfast by Mary. Often it was the first food they had eaten since the previous evening meal. In the afternoon, the students were all taken home after 3.30pm. During the college day, the minibuses were used to drop students off at FE college, on work experience or outward bound sessions.

Donald Macleod ended up working around 30 hours each week.

In his early weeks at Newlands, Macleod picked up Scott [not his real name] at 7.30am from outside a chip shop in Great Western Road. He was parked for a few minutes before the youngster jumped into the side door of the bus.

"How are you doing, Scott?"

"Fuckin' shite," he replied, as he stormed to the rear of the bus.

The vehicle drove off to pick up the next student at Drumchapel. The second student, who was less morose, joined Scott at the back of the bus where they bantered together with some choice language. Macleod had been shocked to learn how disillusioned these young people were about their previous schools. The kids were left bedraggled with no-one interested in them, and no-one giving them any sense of hope.

Macleod found Scott's language aggressive and deplorable.

"Please stop the swearing," said Macleod politely as he drove them towards Newlands.

"Why the fuck, should I bother?"

"Well, if you want to get on with people, you need to adopt a more reasonable tone and people will start to listen to what you have to say," said the ex-polis man.

It took a few more weeks but the minibus relationships grew and Scott was never late or seldom missed a day of college. Scott's parents were decent folks. His profanities continued but he began to modify his language in college. Macleod ended up writing a reference for the student. It was an honest appraisal of a young man learning to control his anger, but the positivity was the student only missed one day in two and half years at junior college when he had a sore throat. Such relationships were very precious. Another anonymous student, who graduated from Newlands and landed a Modern Apprenticeship scheme with Arnold Clark, was grateful.

"I wouldn't be here, Donald, if it wasn't for you," he said.

"What are you talking about, you're a smart boy. You got all your national qualifications," replied the driver/mentor.

"I hadn't been at school for a year before I came to Newlands. I stayed with my Grandmother because both my parents were Drug-addicts. You were there for me every day."

It was not all plain sailing though and there were behavioural issues during transport. In his early weeks at Newlands, a student spat on the floor and windows of the bus and he was pulled up for fighting while Donald Macleod was negotiating Glasgow's nose-to-tail early-morning traffic. The others on the bus sensed Macleod's acute disappointment at their behaviour. They even broke with their own code of 'nae clyping' to explain what had been going on behind the driver's back. The student had used a pair of scissors to rip open the leather seats and pulled out the inner layers of foam. This was beyond the pale.

"I was able to give Philip and Iain a full report about the bus incidents. It was important that the teachers backed up the drivers and did not simply accept the bad behaviour on the way to school."

The young man was immediately suspended from Newlands, a sharp shock which obviously worked.

"After the fighting and vandalism on the bus and then his suspension, I noticed a remarkable change in this boy when he came back," says Macleod.

The ex-police officer set the record straight about the young people who

135

accused the police of harassing them on the housing schemes at night and at the weekend.

> "I'd say don't kid me on, boys. The police really aren't that interested in you but they have to turn out to investigate complaints of anti-social behaviour. They are too busy but they have to because people are phoning up about you. The polis really don't want to chase you, they've got serious stuff to deal with such as assaults, missing persons and firearms situations."

There was a deep realisation that these young people, often acting as hard men, were very vulnerable humans trying to sort out their place in life.

> "A lot of young people think they are so tough and so wide, but it is the exact opposite. They are the least wide, the least tough I've ever met. They don't know how life is," says Macleod.

For Macleod, being able to have a positive impact on their lives was both a privilege and lesson in how these people were able to change.

> "Some of them were changing in front of your eyes. Honestly doing well and really switching on because of the teaching methods, because the ethos of the school and that whole thing coming from Iain and Philip. It was so strong and so different," says Macleod.

Day by day, the Newlands Junior College experience was having an impact.

> "We had one boy who hadn't been in attendance at his mainstream school for over a year. We managed to get that to 100% attendance, without him missing a single day at Newlands Junior College. He is an absolute superstar. He and his big brother live with their Gran," says Orenes.

This student was able to complete his National 5 courses and successfully passed his English and Applications of Mathematics exams. He became a junior college ambassador and visited a major document solutions business in Edinburgh, meeting the firm's managing director, and recounting his experiences with a fellow student.

> "He started as a very shy boy and didn't really talk. Now he has sat his National 5s and passed them all. He was doing practical electronics and he got an apprenticeship with Arnold Clark."

When Elizabeth Orenes was due to take the student to meet a company, she turned up at his mother's address by mistake instead of Gran's home. She phoned to explain she was at the wrong address and running late. Meanwhile, the student was deeply anxious, pacing up and down, presuming no-one was coming for him. On the doorstep, Gran explained when Elizabeth arrived: *"He is so used to being let down by his parents that he thought you weren't going to be there for him either."*

This was the heightened level of attention that was required to break a cycle of truancy and disinterest in education. Everyone involved with the junior college, from Iain White to the drivers and canteen staff, made strenuous efforts to make it difficult for young people not to attend, working to increase their interest and, eventually, leading to a willingness to want to succeed at the college.

CHAPTER EIGHTEEN:
The Human Spirit:
How to Fight Depression and Despair

An incredible insight about the young people at Newlands emerged during an afternoon question and answer session with Scott Black, who was invited to tell a Year One cohort of around 25 about his work.

"Are you a millionaire, Scott?" asked one.

"What kind of car do you drive?" asked another.

"Do you live in a big hoose?" inquired a third.

He tried to field them as best he could, then came a bombshell from a hand at the back.

"Do you ever get depressed?"

Scott Black paused for a moment to consider the gravity of this question.

"I meet hundreds or even thousands of people in my job and I haven't met one person who doesn't get depressed. Everybody gets depressed at some time in life," he replied.

He then turned to Philip, the deputy head, and asked him.

"Philip, do you get depressed."

"Yes," he replied.

Then Black gestured to the young questioner at the back.

"Do you get depressed?"

"Yes, that's why I'm asking the question."

Scott Black asked for a show of hands from the room asking if they got depressed. Every hand shot into the air. Each one of the 13 and 14-year-olds had an experience of depression.

"The thing that I took out of this was not only that they were depressed but that they were prepared to share it. They were just the same as every other adult that I had met," says Black.

He thought back to his own Govan High days and pondered if a teacher asked him if he ever got depressed would he be able to honestly answer.

> "Would I have been able to articulate it, even if I was able to answer it honestly? Probably not."

Black feels this mature discussion within weeks of the students arriving at Newlands proved how far they had come in a short time. This took high levels of trust having such frank conversations in front of a deputy head teacher and a trustee.

Yet the whole sphere of depression, deep anxiety, self-harm and even suicide was not far away from the real lives of many young people at Newlands.

> "I was shocked to find so many young people who have not had safe and happy childhoods. There is trauma and tragedy in their lives that is hard for those from middle-class families to comprehend. They have parents and grandparents who have died and very often have not been shown any depth of love or lasting affection," says Alex Stewart.

He says that what was regularly lost in all his discussions with officials and education professionals was the children: the vulnerable young people who are often just a band of figures and finance and not individuals.

> "Surely, it must be for teachers to say about their work: 'I need to be the difference!' How have we got 14-year-olds in Scotland with reading ages of seven? Everyone wants to blame the secondary schools but it isn't their fault. It is the system all the way back to pre-school," he says.

He says many young people need someone to stand up for them because often parents, grandparents are not able to do so, and this is not always about a lack of love and care.

> "We've got this system where everyone has to be treated equally, even though they don't need it. It's wrong. It has to be child, child, child and not budget, budget, budget."

.....

If one Newlands story exemplifies the fine line between despair and well-being it is about Ross McArthur, who has agreed that we can use his real name. Born in Knightswood on the north side of the Clyde, he was a successful learner at primary school and then attended Knightswood Secondary School, one of the largest secondary schools in Scotland with a roll of 1,400 pupils.

This was out of the official catchment area for Newlands Junior College, seven miles away across the river Clyde.

He finished his first two years at secondary school but his behaviour was becoming more erratic.

"I was in the top class. I was fairly smart and doing OK. But I probably spent more time out of classes than in them. I was being a wee twat," he says.

He does not know why he stopped attending classes at school.

"I just didn't like the whole way we were taught. I couldn't sit in a class and shut up for 30 minutes. I could not do it. At primary school, I was a star kid, then at secondary, it all fell apart. It wasn't to do with the teachers. It was more the friends group that I was in, wasn't the greatest. Some of them were acting up and I tried to copy that and I ended up going from there… Looking back, it wasn't me, but I didn't notice this at the time. I just lost the plot," he recalls. [72]

Ross said he became increasingly sad and depressed and started to mope around in his room all day. He would lie in bed until noon and he wouldn't even come out to eat. "*I stopped doing things that I enjoyed.*"

His mother, Linda, recalls the change.

"He didn't settle well into secondary school: he found the size quite overwhelming, began to struggle with the work, and bullying that had started in primary became more severe. He found that his teachers didn't really know him. Initially, because he was a quiet and well-behaved lad, he became overlooked: unnoticed. At first he was the kind of boy who caused no bother so suffered in silence. However, his behaviour changed and he began to misbehave, to act out. He became quite cheeky and was starting to get into trouble in class."

Ross is mature enough now to see that he was fortunate.

"I had a really good pastoral care teacher and she recommended Newlands. I was one of the only pupils from the North of Glasgow to go to Newlands. At first, I wasn't too keen because I didn't want to leave my friends behind. I wasn't sure how this would work. A lot of the other kids at Newlands knew each other beforehand, whereas I didn't know anybody."

---

72 Ross McArthur interview with the author, January 2020.

His parents were extremely keen for Ross's move but when Newlands asked his school, Knightswood Secondary, to make a contribution to the transport costs, the school raised an objection at the cost of support. There was a temporary stalemate and Ross's mother phoned Philip Graham to raise her complaint.

> "When Ross's Mum phoned us, she was angry and insistent. At first, I thought we were under attack, when she said, 'Your junior college is a postcode lottery and prejudicial. My son cannot get access to your college because of the postcode he lives in. If we lived south of the river, he would have this educational opportunity'. When I came off the phone, I found myself agreeing with her," says Philip Graham.

Ross, stuck in Knightswood, was not heading for a positive future.

> "Having been, by any measure in primary school and early secondary, a model wee guy, getting on at school and loving life, several issues occurred that turned him into a bit of a class clown," says Graham.

The Newlands admissions team spoke with Iain White and they agreed to cover all of the transport costs as part of Ross' scholarship to Newlands. Knightswood's head teacher eventually agreed to the wishes of Ross's parents. Ross started Newlands Junior College in 2017, picked up by the minibus driver each morning. They still keep in touch.

> "So I got to go ... and it changed my life," says Ross.

Gillian Hunt, in her review of Newlands, described the situation.

> "Ross absolutely flourished at Newlands. Although he remained a quiet boy, he made many friends, was mature and could be relied upon. Although academic work was still challenging he began to see real success gaining academic and vocational qualifications. He enjoyed and was inspired by his work experience. His long-term, but so far private (for fear of being bullied about it) interest in politics was now out in the open and growing. He has since been elected to the UK Youth Parliament, the Scottish Youth Parliament and to the Glasgow Youth Council."

When it was time for Ross to graduate from Newlands he had gained all his academic and vocational qualifications, and had attended an interview with Arnold Clark for a business administration apprenticeship. Graduation day for Ross was a mixture of excitement about the future, tinged with sadness at leaving a special place. Philip Graham was delighted for him.

"He had gained so much at NJC: his confidence, qualifications, friends and success in politics but he was moving on from a place he loved. He also felt a little in limbo as he was waiting to hear the outcome of his apprenticeship interview. He didn't have to wait long. As he was called to the stage to graduate it was announced to all that he had been successful in gaining his apprenticeship. There wasn't a dry eye in the house!"

As a post-script, Ross's mother, Linda, speaking at an educational conference in 2021,[73] lamented the demise of the Glasgow establishment: *"People said Newlands Junior College was like a family and that's what it was. It was like a family! There were no barriers and I think it is a tragic shame that it's not there now because it has transformed lives."*

---

73 Reform Scotland's Commission on School Reform: "Engaging the Disengaged – Alternative Approaches to Education", 21 January 2021.

CHAPTER NINETEEN:

On the Road to Success: A Future with Arnold Clark

Ross McArthur was not an isolated success story. The results were nothing short of astonishing. The junior college had been designed to support disengaged students, those who may have ended up furthest from the labour market, young people lost from the education system, destined to end up unemployed at the age of 16, without much hope for their futures. The college's success in preparing them for jobs, through a vocationally-focused educational experience, was beyond everyone's wildest expectation.

Students selected a minimum of three vocational options from a choice of ten and completed qualifications in those. These were sourced from City of Glasgow College, GTG Training (Arnold Clark) and Riverside Music Complex, where students learned about making music and recording techniques, with attendance at those locations. The relationship between the providers of vocational opportunities and the college was a key facet of each success story.

Bespoke courses were devised for students and developed in partnership with the individual. Collaboration and constant dialogue were crucial and this meant weekly, sometimes daily, contact between the junior college and the outside partner.

Work experience became a critical aspect of the college's success and was massively popular. A Year One student, from the 2017 and 2018 cohort, completing a week's work placement at an Arnold Clark garage, concluded: *"This has been the best week of my life. When can I go back?"*

The guarantee of an apprenticeship in a real workplace or a positive destination after the junior college was its attainable pot of gold at the end of the educational rainbow. And the students knew this was their chance. Another student called Thomas, not his real name, said:

"When I was at a 'normal' school I was annoying, disruptive, never in class (sometimes dogging it, sometimes outside). I was always in trouble. I didn't take school life seriously — especially in S1 and S2

143

— and saw every day as a joke, a chance to carry on and have a laugh. I really did try to change at the end of S3 but by then the teachers disliked me and had stopped giving me the chances they had given me in my first two years. It was too late to prove I could be someone else."

He explained if he had stayed at that school, he would never have had an opportunity to undertake work experience because no-one trusted him to behave. Furthermore, he would not be allowed to take part in Outward Bound courses.

"I behaved the way I did because I thought school was a joke and now that I have learned about the importance of work experience, I now understand why school is important to my future." [74]

It was a familiar story. In a Newlands student yearbook, Qasim Bilal wrote:

"In my old school, I used to mess about in class but then I got nominated for Newlands Junior College, and I felt happy, and knew I was very lucky. My pastoral care teacher gave me information about NJC and told me 'not to mess about.' On my first day at NJC I was shy and took two or three weeks before I made friends. Now I am confident going to College, I have friends and don't skip classes. I didn't know that learning was so important, but I do now, and am trying my best to learn, especially to read, write and listen."

Qasim Bilal enjoyed construction and engineering projects and wanted to become an engineer when he left the junior college. He was one of the students who was taken on day-release at Arnold Clark and given extra-curricular activities to experience practical work in a motor workshop.

"By no means did we take the whole class to our training school to teach them about motor mechanics. If they were really interested, we would take a cohort of about ten and 15. Once they experienced the work, they either liked it or didn't think it was for them. This then came down to a core of between three and five people who were very keen," says Eddie Hawthorne. "Provided they were getting their qualifications, we would offer them an apprenticeship," he says.

---

74 Ibid, Gillian Hunt, 2020.

In November 2018, Qasim, who graduated from NJC in 2016, returned to Newlands on his new motor cycle. After graduation, he did secure an apprenticeship with Arnold Clark and Alex Stewart was delighted for this young man, giving him a Facebook thumbs up and a '*Nice wheels*' comment.

Work experience was provided by supportive employers, working in partnership with the junior college. The positive approach and culture ensured that this was a key element and due to the size of the junior college it was able to be adaptive, flexible and agile in organising this for students.

Developing the Young Workforce Career Education Standard (3-18) states that it is the aim, "*to achieve better connectivity and cooperation between education and the world of work to ensure that young people at all levels of education understand the expectation of employer, and that employers are properly engaged.*"

This vocational exposure opened the door for Edan Harley, another Newlands alumni who works with Arnold Clark and was happy to be mentioned by name in this book. Edan lived in Govanhill in the south side of Glasgow and attended Holyrood Secondary School, a Roman Catholic school in Dixon Road. Its vision statement is that it is a '*safe and nurturing environment where we work together to ensure all young people have an equal chance to reach their fullest potential.*' A powerful aspiration. Furthermore, the school's parent council annual meeting in August 2018 reported pupils in S4 had attained the best set of results the school has seen, and that there was a "huge reduction" in those who did not achieve 5 at National 3. It stated the school wanted "to try to engage better for level 3 from 4 to 5…. Overall an outstanding performance in S4". [75] By all accounts, Holyrood's staff work extremely hard for the majority of its school pupils.

However, some do slip through the cracks. Edan attended some classes because they were 'fine' for him but there were certain others he disliked because of the teacher or the subject. He was actually in school every day yet skipping a regular class where the teacher thought he was off for eight weeks. Why was this?

> "When you go to school the teachers they just shouted at you, you don't get any respect," he says.

Increasingly, Edan skipped classes, skiving off to get something to eat in local chip shops and kebab outlets, passing time with others who had dodged

---

75 Holyrood RC Secondary School Parent Council AGM, 28th August 2018.

classes. He sat five prelim exams and failed them all. This was a young person definitely heading in the wrong direction.

> "I was going to go to Newlands in the year when it opened but I was in trouble at school. They wouldn't let me go. I went to school for two years but after that I never went to school. Around third year, I just stopped going." [76]

> "We all felt the same about school and drifted away and didn't really go. It was not a question of 'Are we going to school', it was a question of 'Are we gonna skip it today or are we going to go in? We didn't really bother."

One of Edan's friends was sent on a scholarship to Newlands. He heard from him how different it was and this encouraged Edan to think about applying. Edan admits he became annoyingly persistent, frequently hassling his year head, Margaret Leyden, if he could go.

> "I used to ask her every second day. I hated school. She kept saying, 'No, you're not going and 'Why do you want to go there so much?' It will gie me a better education than I'm getting here,' was my reply."

Margaret Leyden, a critical friend of Newlands, was exasperated by the pupil's persistence, telling him he was at one of the best schools in Europe and should make the most of this. However, she considered the young person's plea and phoned Philip Graham.

> "She knew me from working at Glasgow City Council and realised we weren't international child smugglers. She said she understood what kind of pupil we were looking for. 'I've got this boy, but I just don't know if he's cut out for this, if he's ready. Under normal circumstances, I would have nominated him but he's just on the edge'," recalls Graham.

Eventually, Leyden took the plunge, completed a Nomination Form and Edan Harley was interviewed and, to Graham, came across as an *"articulate and positive young man who had, rather unusually, a very clear idea of where he wanted to end up."*

Edan Harley started at Newlands in 2015. He arrived by taxi at 8.15am on his first day but later the minibus picked him up at an agreed spot. Phil Graham cast a beady eye over this new admission.

---

76 Edan Harley interview with the author, January 2020.

"If you knew what was motivating Edan, you would say, 'OK, I hear what you are saying'."

While Edan was still trying to determine what he wanted from life, he was clear that it meant good employment and the prospect of working his way up.

"I wanted to get into a job and try and do better than I'd done before," he says.

Edan's friend had told him that all he needed to do was apply himself to the work and activities at the junior college, and he would get on well.

"They break you in a bit and give you the easy stuff to see how good you are at it. Then they know what work to give you after the first assessments," he recalls.

He ended up taking Higher English, which at one point was unattainable for him, and was proud of his attendance record.

"It was completely different. I wouldn't miss a day at Newlands. One of my best friends at secondary school went to Newlands: we used to skip school all the time, but when we went to Newlands, both years, we had a 100% attendance."

How does he explain this dramatic change in behaviour?

"Because you enjoy going. If you don't like something, you're not going to do it. It's something you want to do. If you enjoy something, you're gonna go."

What was so enjoyable about Newlands?

"I think it was the flexibility. You didn't get shouted at. Even if you walked in late, maybe ten or 15 minutes late, nobody even questioned it, and you weren't going to be shouted at. All these things about, 'I'm gonna be late because I haven't got a pen or a pencil'. All these worries that they give you, you don't need to bother with all that. It's no a big deal if you don't have a pen. Newlands was so flexible, nobody was going to moan at you for things."

He settled in well and made many friends.

"Quite quickly, you are friends with everyone, even although you might not talk to everyone all of the time. In general, we all got on with everyone. Everyone had a laugh with each other."

This constant encouragement made Edan realise he was capable of doing a great deal more with his life, taking control of his development as a young person. By June 2017, he had visited a number of workplaces, including a week's work experience at Arnold Clark in the mechanics workshop.

> "I enjoyed it. I thought it was great. But to be a manager you needed to undertake a three-year apprenticeship, and I didn't like it that much to do it for that length of time. I applied for different places, such as BAE Systems, but didn't see anything I really liked."

Edan was being mentored by Alex Stewart on a one-to-one basis, every Tuesday at 2pm for an hour. Stewart arranged for Edan to meet Eddie Hawthorne before a trustee meeting.

> "I was really impressed that someone who was in charge of such a major company would have the time to come and meet me. He was a very busy man yet he made the time," explains Edan.

Hawthorne set out the options: become an apprentice mechanic before qualifying as a workshop manager, or work in customer sales and climb up on the commercial and sales side. Customer service appealed more to Edan and it meant that he could work in customer services, including the complaints department, while he learned to drive a car and pass his driving test.

When he left Newlands in June 2017, he joined Arnold Clark in sales. Speaking in 2020, after two and a half years in the job, he says: "*It was Newlands that gave me that hope. I have a vision that I want to be a future manager and maybe, one day, the boss. If I hadn't gone to Newlands I wouldn't have had that positive and open mindset in me.*"

CHAPTER TWENTY:
A Stream of VIPs Take Note

Newlands Junior College was in the news. Despite the distinct lack of enthusiasm from the directorate in Glasgow City Council's Education Services, others were wishing the pilot well. Almost every other day, there were visitors streaming through the front door to meet the students and staff. Iain White was delighted to welcome them and show them around, and as with his time at Govan, let the visitors have uninterrupted time speaking with the young people.

Scotland's First Minister, Nicola Sturgeon, visited the junior college on Friday, 18th March 2016, piped in by Jamie Barbour, playing *Rowan Tree* with Govan Schools Pipe Band. She stayed for a working lunch with the students and heard more about the success from various people. She was very relaxed and shared a Face Swap app with a couple of students, including Megan Lynch, and Jim McColl which caused great hilarity. The relations between First Minister and Jim McColl were cordial and the SNP leader appeared to be genuinely impressed with the young people, who were excited about her arrival.

As 2016 progressed, the junior college was delighted to welcome the Deputy First Minister and Education Secretary, John Swinney, who came on Thursday, 1st September 2016. He had been a big supporter of the concept and a champion of the idea within the Scottish Government in Edinburgh, and now he witnessed it in action.

> "It was a pleasure for me to be there when John Swinney visited. I could see that he was deeply impressed by what had been achieved. The students on the day were exemplars for the whole idea. I'm sure it will have stuck in the mind of Mr Swinney and the other guests that day," recalls McColl.

Swinney was accompanied by Lesley Johnston, of the HMI Inspectorate, Sir Harry Burns, the Chief Medical Officer for Scotland, and Susan Dalziel, one of the parents. Also among the notable visitors was Paul Little, Principal and chief executive of City of Glasgow College, which was collaborating with the junior college on admissions. In January 2020, Mr Little was elected as the President of Glasgow Chamber of Commerce.

> "I was very supportive of the Newlands Junior College concept. Iain White, Jim McColl and all the staff created something very special and we, at City of Glasgow College, were delighted to work as partners to the junior college," says Mr Little.[77]

Several students went from Newlands on to full-time courses at City of Glasgow College studying construction [and women in construction], joinery, music technology, hairdressing, hospitality, computing and photography.

The operation of the junior college garnered serious political interest from all parties. In the following weeks and months, Jim Sillars, the veteran Scottish nationalist politician, came and shared his experiences, along with Stewart McDonald, the local Glasgow South MP, and a former pupil of Govan High, while Willie Rennie, the leader of the Scottish Liberal Democrats, Liz Smith, the Scottish Conservative's education spokesperson, and Iain Gray, the Labour Party education and skills spokesperson, all listened with interest to the views of the young people.

On 30th January, 2017 Ruth Davidson, the then leader of the Scottish Conservative, visited. *"She was very supportive. She was scheduled to come in for an hour and stayed for a couple of hours,"* says McColl. Her message after visiting was:

> "On a visit to Newlands Junior College this morning we called for the Scottish Government to get behind community efforts to promote vocational education. After years of under-performance and a persistent attainment gap, Scotland's failed one-size-fits-all education system needs reform."

The Scottish Parliament debated education and training in early January 2018, when it considered the Wood Report on developing the young workforce, with Newlands mentioned among others in glowing terms.[78]

The Scottish Minister for Employability and Training Jamie Hepburn, referring to Scotland's Year of Young People, made it clear the Scottish Government was making a priority of education and *"our on-going commitment to equip our young people with the skills and qualifications that they need to succeed in a rapidly changing labour market."*

Liz Smith, the Conservative MSP, explained that Newlands had been a hugely successful institution, supporting young people between the ages of 14 and

---

77 Interview with the author, March 2020.
78 Scottish Parliament debate, 11 January 2018. www.parliament.scot/parliamentarybusiness/report.aspx?r=11299&i=102836&c=2054816&s=Newlands

16 who have been disengaged from mainstream education but have found their niche at the college.

"I listen carefully to what Jim McColl says, whether it is in his articles for *The Herald* or when I meet him, as I have done on a couple of occasions, and the Newlands example is part of that diversity. The calls for similar institutions across Scotland should not be left unheard, because that diversity is important—it motivates young people. That is plain for all to see when they visit Newlands Junior College, which deserves a great deal of credit for what it has done in providing that diversity. The strong messages from Ian Wood and from institutions such as Newlands are important."

The local Newlands MSP, James Dornan, an SNP member, also spoke up for the junior college in the same debate.

"I will mention Newlands Junior College, as Liz Smith did in her speech. It is in my constituency and I have visited it a few times. I have spoken to Mr McColl and others, and the college is a very good example of how people from difficult circumstances who find school and education difficult on the whole can move on and make a difference to their lives. I thank Liz Smith for mentioning it."

At this juncture, the junior college was enjoying support and plaudits from all sides of the Scottish Parliament in Edinburgh. Word was getting out among young people who were being nominated for the college. During the assessment interviews in May 2018 a candidate was asked: "*What do you know about NJC already?*" He replied that, as well as researching the Facebook page, reading information given to him by his guidance teacher and watching a YouTube video, he also knew current and former students and they had told him that NJC was "*Sound!*" That was proper peer-group endorsement, felt the teaching staff.

While the coffee morning run by students was a hit with the local community, the college was ambitious to show off its work to potential backers. The fund raising committee, decided to hold 'A Night at the College' on Monday, 20th February 2017.

While this was a fantastic night with the students putting on an exceptional show of their activities, the college trustees were disappointed because they only managed to secure one extra donor.

"We tried a fundraiser at the college. We explained to the students that the college needed to raise money to keep going and it would be good if they could think of ways of getting involved," says Black.

Gillian Hunt, who attended was also impressed with the evening, but thought the pitch for funding was perhaps too low-key.

"At the evening, it was very soft selling. I think looking back it was a missed opportunity. The junior college should have been more up-front about it, making a real 'ask' of people who attended. They could have said pledging a certain amount of money would guarantee a place for a student, but they were just too nice about it."

.....

One young man who became a powerful ambassador for the college, helping with fundraising and meeting many influential people was Peter Gordon. In 2017, the junior college was recognised as a finalist in the Postcode Lottery awards. The potential pot of prize money was £500,000. Peter was involved in a workshop with the judging panel, including senior representatives from Virgin Money. The junior college's bid was backed by Business in the Community Scotland and its director Alan Thornburrow, who became the college's partner in the application. In all, it was an amazing effort with Newlands' submission down to the final five from 224 applications. Unfortunately, it was pipped in the final round by a charity supporting dogs which can find missing persons.

Peter Gordon was an energetic young man with entrepreneurial genes in his body from an early age. According to Philip Graham, the youngster had experienced a terrible time at both home and school before coming to Newlands. "*He was heading for real challenges until he joined us*," he says.

When he arrived at the junior college, his positive potential was unleashed with verve and gusto. He wanted to help. There was a report log for repairs when something was needing fixed or repaired. Peter would do his best to try and fix it first, often saving the college a call-out and repair fee from a professional. When it was suggested they might save money by cleaning its minibus, Peter helped raise the money for an outdoor tap and a steam cleaner, and he contacted the tradesman to negotiate a better price.

"He was absolutely flying. He was running two businesses outside as well: one doing gardening and another doing a car wash. He was just 16. He sat National 4s and 5s which were not on the horizon at his previous school. He would have left with nothing. He eventually managed to secure an apprenticeship at Arnold Clark," says Gillian Hunt.

There was some irony in this transformation. A representative of the City of Edinburgh Council visited the junior college. He was welcomed by Peter Gordon who took him on a guided tour. He obviously impressed the guest. Afterwards, while having tea with Iain White, the guest from the Capital commented that Newlands was obviously not really a place for kids with problems. White nearly coughed into his teacup.

> "The young man who has just shown you around, wouldn't have been in that position and able to articulate in that way two years ago. It is Newlands Junior College which has encouraged him and brought it out of him," declared White.

This was a typical issue when visitors came to view the junior college: they simply did not appreciate the background of the young people and how much they had changed and progressed once they stepped over the threshold.

Another powerful junior college ambassador is Lisa Kane. She was born in Glasgow at the Queen Elizabeth Hospital and brought up in Pollok. She attended St Bernard's RC Primary School in Dove Street, Pollok, and then went on to St Paul's High School, a co-educational Roman Catholic secondary school, in Damshot Road, with a maximum role of 950 pupils. Both schools are in the G53 region, one of the most deprived postcodes of SIMD (Scottish Index of Multiple Deprivation). Lisa's Mum moved to Motherwell and her Dad died. Since the age of seven, she was living with her Aunt Helen, her Dad's sister, and her little sister. Helen had a partner at the time but after he left it was just the three in the house. Lisa was in third year at high school before going to Newlands in 2017. According to 2019 figures, there were 178 pupils in secondary three, 195 in secondary four, dropping to 110 for secondary five, and 58 for sixth year. In 2020, there were 1,074 pupils. This was a big city school where it was easy to get lost. [79]

Lisa had been good academically but had stopped going to school. She was 15.

> "I got bullied. The thing that made me not want to go to school was I was attacked. Then the teachers made out that I was bullying the girl that attacked me."[80]

However, Lisa's school discouraged any suggestion she might go elsewhere to learn.

> "St Paul's didn't like it because they thought if people heard about

79 St Paul's High School, Facts and Figures. 2020. www.st-paulshigh.glasgow.sch.uk/PlainText/PlainText.aspx?SectionId=6c410996-4c5f-4600-ae20-f72c27f70a4c
80 Lisa Kane interview with the author, January 2020.

pupils having to be removed for certain reasons, it would give the school a bad reputation. So they didn't even bring it up."

The daughter of the woman at her Aunt's work was attending Newlands, and her Aunt heard that there had been a difference in the girl since she's moved there. Her attitude and her work has been so much better.

"Like, she comes home and tidies her house up and her manners were better to her Mum and stuff," says Lisa.

Phil Graham remembers receiving the application from Lisa's school.

"Her application was very straight-forward. There was a very positive application from the school. Lisa was not terribly sure about coming to the college but she had a reason to get a fresh start and put a lot of things behind her," he says.

According to the admissions team, they thought that Lisa should be happy and performing well in school.

"She was not our regular 'customer'. We said we would take her to the next stage but we were convinced that Lisa herself would decide if it wasn't for her."

She walked in through the front door at lunch-time at nomination stage.

"She was different and everyone looked up from their work as she approached," recalls Phil Graham.

Her first impression was the college resembled the Glasgow Science Centre, a concrete and glass building on the River Clyde, which is used to encourage young people to take up careers in science and technology. It was an acute observation.

"It was painted white and clean. My school was old and dull yet this place was bright and it made me feel happier. The atmosphere was different and I could tell this before I even met any of the other people," she says.

Apart from a student in the year below, Lisa did not know anyone and found the first moments of junior college nerve-wracking.

"When I'm really nervous in a situation, I think 'Will it improve my future?' If I think it will, then I just push on with it. I need to get on with it, because I know it will do me good. That's what I was thinking. I made friends quickly. There were only a few girls but I made friends with everybody at the college eventually."

After her first few days, she was picked up each morning near a railway bridge between Priesthill and Darnley at 8.30am, and she was given breakfast at the college. Lisa settled in and was able to make the most of this opportunity. Today, she is on a positive career trajectory. She has become an exemplar and remains a committed advocate of the junior college, when she could so easily have taken a different path in life.

.....

There is a postscript here. Many Newlands alumni were so proud of their connection with the junior college, they wanted to help it succeed, so others might benefit. In June 2018, Peter Gordon volunteered to return and help with the summer refurbishment. The college's Facebook post declared: *"There are some special people in the history of Newlands Junior College. This guy deserves a special mention. After ONE year of his scholarship, he has secured an apprenticeship with Arnold Clark. Peter has, in a short space of time, taken responsibility for his own learning, his career, has pro-actively sought out his own apprenticeship and not only that, but he took over the maintenance and repair of so many things around the college, washed and valeted the minibuses (and staff cars!), encouraged other students who were struggling and also represented students on the student council and presented to funding boards and the Board of Trustees.*

What you know about this young man is a fraction of the whole story, but his story is incredible. He has always asked what he can do for NJC and not once - NOT ONCE - asked what NJC can do for him. He will be joining us all through summer on work experience in the building, repairing and maintaining, as he "doesn't want to get into trouble over the summer".

Is Peter perfect? Nope. He - like all of us - has a lot of learning still to do. He has many things that he needs to work on and improve. He is a long way from the end of his journey. But if he continues to listen and continues to learn, there is no saying where he might be."

Peter and Philip Graham undertook the work together and the former student finished off the painting work in the social area with coats of emulsion, glossed the skirting in the boys' toilet and also tightened the loose taps in the toilet. This story remains an incredibly powerful endorsement of Newlands.

CHAPTER TWENTY-ONE:

So How Was the College Doing?

Jim McColl was clear that the college needed proper educational and vocational evaluation if it was going to prove its worth to the wider world. It was then that former teacher Gillian Hunt became part of the Newlands Junior College story.

She is an educational consultant based in Edinburgh. She had been employed by City of Edinburgh Council in the Education Department and she decided to become a freelance consultant in April 2016.

> "Up until this point I was an educator. I was a teacher for the first half of my career, a primary teacher then a senior manager in primary schools until 2001. For the second half of my career, I was a senior manager at Edinburgh Council leading learning and development," she says.[81]

In between, she became a senior lecturer and programme director of the chartered teachers programme at the University of Edinburgh, before returning to Edinburgh Council in 2004.

> "I missed it. I loved being part of the council when I was there. I went back as a manager of the team of around 24 where I had worked previously, as the leadership development officer. At that time, we had a significant budget for training," she explains.

She held this position for 12 years, leading the team supporting the learning and development of teachers, community learning workers and later those in social work.

> "I loved being a teacher but my job with the council became further and further removed from children and families as we worked to help teachers. Latterly, I felt I was purely a manager of money, which wasn't my strong point."

But it was her experience working for five years, from 2009 until 2014, on the Children's Panel which opened her eyes to what was happening to young people in certain communities in Scotland.

---

81 Gillian Hunt interview with the author, January 2020.

"Actually experiencing what was going on for children in our city [Edinburgh] and finding out what had gone wrong for kids on our watch was shocking. I was disappointed and I felt a responsibility for it."

It was then that she met Chris Kilkenny, who was then 15 years old. Chris, who had been in care, was speaking on behalf of WhoCaresScotland. He explained how difficult it was to get a house, and how that the council's leisure facilities were beyond the finances of looked-after children and their carers.

Kilkenny was able to influence the city's chief executive Sue Bruce to make significant changes in terms of inclusion for looked-after children and their carers to get leisure access cards. In 2017, Hunt met with Kilkenny, now 21, when he spoke about poverty, about how he was in rehab twice before the age of 11 with his mother due to her heroin addiction, and time spent in care homes.

"It was a Eureka moment. Chris had been in the system since I was a teacher and senior manager working in the council. He talked about what it was like living in poverty. I realised I still hadn't managed to make a proper difference to his life. I was appalled."

Hunt knew Iain White through the Scottish Educational Leadership, Management and Administration Society (SELMAS), an independent organisation providing the context and stimulus for thinking about the big educational issues in Scotland. Its aim was to engage educational leaders in relevant social issues, provoking debate among educationists. It was *a safe space for a candid expression of views*".

In September 2008, Iain White was a presenter along with Fiona Hyslop, MSP, Cabinet Secretary for Education and Lifelong Learning, at the conference in Stirling Management Centre, with Gillian Hunt in the attendance. Several years later, in November 2015, Chris Kilkenny was invited to speak at the SELMAS forum in Edinburgh, while Jim McColl was also a speaker talking about Newlands Junior College on the same bill. He was followed by Gerry Lyons, head teacher of St Andrew's Secondary School, at Carntyne in Glasgow, who would become a central figure in the decision about the future of Newlands.

In a 2015 conference blog, SELMAS committee member Jayne Horsburgh commented: *"Care leaver, ex young carer and now poverty campaigner,*

Chris Kilkenny's experience, in a society which prides itself on providing free education for all, provided a real wake up call." Chris explained how his choices at school were limited because there was no money in the family to pay for things like home economics and school trips.

> "Without blame or self-pity, Chris articulated how it really is and what really can make a difference to a young person in poverty. His solutions were not sweeping policy changes or grandiose schemes but a considered plea to simply care. Care about the young people in your class, school and community."

Horsburgh continued:

> "Jim McColl has certainly taken that challenge personally and is currently making a real difference to the lives of the young people who now attend Newlands Junior College, Glasgow. Seeking to close the 'opportunity gap' for 'young people who are trapped' in the poverty cycle, Jim echoed Chris's plea for relationship building with the young people and their families, challenging the lack of parity between vocational and academic education. While I admire this initiative and am grateful that someone is indeed doing his bit to make a difference, it seems to me unfortunate that Jim has had to develop an independent school in order to achieve this. Perhaps GIRFEC [Getting it right for every child] really means that there is a need to provide more appropriate provision to meet the needs of our young people in more diverse ways and not maintain what we have been guilty of in recent years i.e. an interpretation of inclusion which forces the impossible on comprehensive schools, expecting them to be 'all things to all men' and recognising that one size will not fit all!"

After the conference, Kilkenny was invited to visit Newlands Junior College in Glasgow, speaking with students and the staff. In May 2018, two of Newlands alumni, Giancarlo Pelosi and Edan Harley, both now employed and doing well at Arnold Clark, spoke at the SELMAS Forum dinner, and made a major impact.

As the Christmas holidays of 2018 approached, the junior college was settled and doing well. Everyone connected with the establishment was pleased with the performance, and the omens looked good for 2019, when critical decisions about the future were expected.

There were now 46 students at the college. Year One group had 25, which was three more than in September. It peaked at 26 but one student had their scholarship withdrawn. Year Two had 21 students, one less than in September because a student reached the statutory school leaving age and decided to go.

Victoria Rose, who replaced the original English teacher Samantha Wrigglesworth, stepped down and Graham Robertson took over. All students were working on essay writing and close reading skills. In Year One, eight students were working towards National 3. Robertson also ramped up the college's connection with The Pacific Institute which was helping to inform the ethos of the college. Every college staff member, and trustee Alex Stewart, was trained in the TPI principles encouraging positive psychology and goal-setting. All students attended the PX2 course, a step-by-step process using the Organisational Culture Inventory tool, while one-to-one mentoring became a vital part of personal development. This "pioneering approach to education" was recognised by TPI which presented Newlands Junior College with the first award and commendation of its kind at the 2018 Graduation, with a plaque commemorating and celebrating the special relationship.

In March 2017, Dr Lindsay Paterson, the respected educationist and professor of education policy at Edinburgh University, said Scotland still had a poor record on training and was not very good at vocational skills.[82]

> "There are a few islands of practice in Scotland that might encourage hope that these ideas could find some welcome here. A notable one is Newlands Junior College in Glasgow, set up by the industrialist Jim McColl in partnership with the local authorities in the area. It aims to teach young people in their mid-teenage years who are seriously disaffected from school. Crucial to that is indeed the preparation of technical skills," he wrote.

.....

Scotland's national statistics revealed that only 75% of all 16-year-old school leavers in Scotland in 2018 gained a 'positive destination'. The predicted situation for new Newlands' students was not even as positive, as students' previous schools estimated that only about 25% might gain positive outcomes.

Over its five years of operation, 134 students attended Newlands Junior College, with 19 students returning to local authority schools for a variety of reasons. A very small number had their scholarship withdrawn for disciplinary reasons, others simply withdrew (in some cases having failed to engage with NJC for more than the briefest period).

---

82 The Sunday Times, 12 March 2017.

It is not known whether these students entered positive destinations as Newlands was never updated about their progress. At the time of the junior college's closure, 26 students returned to local authority schools to complete their statutory education as they were not yet 16.

Here is the statistic which exemplifies the success story. Of the 89 students who completed their education at Newlands, 92.1% went on to a positive destination, designated as a further education college course, an apprenticeship or a full-time job. This, by any measurement, is an outstanding achievement. If we include the 19 students mentioned above who had some contact with NJC but returned to local authority schools, and make an assumption that they did not attain a positive outcome, then 75.9% of 108 students went onto a positive destination.

The students at Newlands had closer links to employment as work experience was the ignition key to switching students on to possible future careers. Graham Robertson was developing ever stronger links between the junior college and a raft of business employers. It was essential that students gained a positive and realistic experience. In these extended work experience placements students began to understand the world of work and were given the opportunity to grow into being an employee. Increasingly, the students were becoming work-ready.

A similar tale can be told about application and attendance at the further education college. Because the young people spent three half days a week at an FE college during their two years at Newlands, they knew what college was like and what was expected. Again, they were able to grow into being full-time FE students. It was not always plain sailing and student behaviour — and levels of maturity — certainly posed some early concerns for the FE colleges. However, it is widely accepted that many 16 year-olds coming straight from school do not cope with attendance at FE college and the drop-out rate is high. Newlands students were well supported and eventually college-ready

In early 2018, Jim McColl was giving evidence to a Scottish Parliament committee on investment and the development of the Scottish economy. As one of the panellist, he was asked by the committee member Tom Arthur, SNP MSP for Renfrewshire South, to speak about inclusive growth.[83] His reply was stark.

---

83 Economy, Jobs and Fair Work Committee, Scottish Parliament, 20 January 2018. www.parliament.scot/parliamentarybusiness/report.aspx?r=11342&i=103192&c=2061288&s=Jim%2520McColl

"That is a pet subject of mine. We have an excluded group in the areas of multiple deprivation in our bigger cities such as Edinburgh, Glasgow and Dundee. Taking Glasgow as an example, I note that 700 young people a year leave school at the statutory leaving age, 50% of whom will go into jobs or go to college, so they are motivated. Thirty per cent will get involved with Skills Development Scotland or activity events. Schools are allowed to put a tick against that and say that it is a positive destination. It is positive in that the young people are engaging with the support, but it is not a positive destination. The figures that we get cover that up a bit. Beyond that, 20% disappear off the radar. They do not engage with any public support, and that is the poverty trap. It happens every year, and the statistics are the same in Edinburgh and Dundee, which are the two other cities that I have tested. The pattern repeats consistently. That is a large number of young people who are being trapped in poverty, and we do not do anything about it. To me, inclusive growth is about giving those young people, who are talented but who maybe do not fit into the academic system, the training, opportunities and education that fits them. We should be engaging them in a way in which they will engage."

McColl went on to say this frustration was the reason he started Newlands Junior College, which he said has been "hugely successful".

"We have had 100% success in young people going into work or going to college — 100% real jobs and real college places. This is the fourth year of the college. The Cabinet Secretary for Education and Skills is supporting it in some way. My real problem is the local authority. I have another meeting with the leader of Glasgow City Council this afternoon. It is letting these young people down."

McColl then went on to talk about what inclusive growth, one of the key tenets of the Scottish Government, meant for him.

"We talk about attainment as being five Highers or more at a certain grade. We need those young people in the skills base as technicians, but we are not investing in them. I gave an example to the Council of Economic Advisers. We teach Tommy from Toryglen — an area of multiple deprivation in Glasgow. We invest four years of secondary education in him at £7,600 a year. Two years are wasted because he stops attending after two years; he is absent. We invest in Nigel from

161

Newton Mearns, which is a posh part of Glasgow, with six years of secondary education and four years of university education, so Nigel gets more support than wee Tommy. Wee Tommy is not worth the additional support, yet it is not a big additional amount of money. To me, inclusive growth is about taking care of those people at the bottom. It is not about trying to push more people through a system that caters only for the majority. It caters for them in a good way, but we are leaving too many young people behind, and that is not inclusive."

McColl's message resonated well beyond the committee room in Edinburgh. He concluded by explaining:

"I called Newlands a 'junior college' so that it did not have the stigma of a special school. It takes people at 14; they are already out on the streets at that age, but if you can give them an alternative you have a better chance of saving them. I do not think that there is enough support at that point. A lot goes on, but the sort of thing that goes on is maybe a six-week course. Six-weeks is not long enough to make an impact on these young peoples' lives."

He said the junior college was trying to deal with people coming from troubled backgrounds, who have been abused mentally and sometimes physically for years. Many were from disruptive homes and they were not healthy.

"We pick them up in the morning, give them breakfast and take them to college. We tie up with the local colleges three half-days a week, to give them a choice of three vocational skills and get them interested in something."

But McColl wanted the MSPs on the parliamentary committee to understand he had no ambition to be in the education sector for the long haul.

"To make it clear, I do not want to be in education. I think that what we do should be part of the public sector, with the private sector in local areas getting involved and contributing. It needs to be part of the public sector. I worry that because we have done what we do, people will think that they do not need to help. It cannot work if it is done by the private sector; it has to be part of the education system of Scotland," he concluded.

Nothing could be clearer than this statement: McColl wanted the public sector to step up and sort this.

162

CHAPTER TWENTY-TWO:

Deal or No Deal:
Council Pulls Plug on Transition Plan

In May 2017, the Scottish National Party won control of the city of Glasgow. It now had the levers of primary and secondary education in its hands. With John Swinney, as SNP Education Minister, this appeared to bode well for Newlands. The new council leader Susan Aitken had promised voters that the city would not be run by its council officials.

The new Nationalist broom swept in by castigating the Labour Party cabal for the years of misrule in the city. The Scottish National Party's city leadership promised to do so much more, and the voting public in Scotland's largest city were strongly behind them.

> "At every juncture, John Swinney at least tried to help the college's development. He turned up and filled in some of the vacuum left by local government. We were under the impression we would get £7,600 per pupil from somewhere from the public sector and the private sector would be making up the rest. We also knew the private sector would be putting our money where our mouths were," says Stewart.

During the summer of 2017, McColl met Aitken, the new leader, and was heartened to hear her initial commitment. "She was very supportive of the school when she was elected," says McColl, speaking in 2019.[84]

On 21st June 2017, the Scottish Government, using their powers under the Standards in Scotland's Schools provision, offered Newlands Junior College, a grant of £345,000, which was conditional on securing match funding from local government.

The junior college's official grant submission in March explaining the funding rationale asked for some draw-down of this money saying they already had a level of match-funding from Glasgow and Renfrewshire Council. Eventually, the Scottish Government paid out around £300,000 for 2018 and 2019, with a final instalment, around £62,000 delayed when there were concerns over the future.

---

84 Jim McColl interview with the author, May 2019.

From Newlands Junior College's standpoint, it became a battle each year to extract the agreed money from the council. In negotiations, Alex Stewart explained there had been a five-year commitment to the pilot from the previous council leader, yet the new council claimed no such agreement existed. Stewart was forced to find the letter to prove that it had been sent.

> "We got the original grant confirmed in a letter from the council and we felt that the negotiations would continue. What we didn't know was that it became a brick wall and, in the fourth year of our operations, Glasgow even tried to say they were not doing it anymore. I wasn't fully involved at the time, but I had to find that original letter," explains Stewart.

The council did pay the £100,000 commitment made by the previous council leaders, but it was the kind of feet-dragging and deliberate obfuscation which wore down the college trustees.

> "I was constantly saying to council officials that this was a collaborative venture and that we were in this together. It never truly felt like this," adds Stewart.

In April 2018, McColl, after giving his evidence to the Scottish Parliament's Economy, Jobs and Fair Work Committee, met the Chief Executive of Glasgow Council, Annemarie O'Donnell, to seek a commitment for an orderly transition the following year.

By all accounts, the meeting was cordial and there was a belief that Newlands Junior College would have a long-term and sustained future within Glasgow's range of educational options. McColl was deeply encouraged by the response.

> *Dear Annemarie*
>
> *Thank you for taking the time to meet with me on Wednesday and for the very constructive discussion on the future of Newlands Junior College. I was very pleased to hear of your commitment to integrate the college and its key values into the Glasgow education system and your intention to create between three to five facilities around Glasgow. We agreed to put together a transition team with a view to passing over the responsibility of the college to the Council in August 2019. I have spoken to Alex Stewart and Keir Bloomer about the transition and they have agreed to be our two nominees for the transition team. It would be good to have a kick-off meeting fairly*

soon. Please let me know your thoughts on timings. Thanks once again for the constructive meeting.

Best wishes

Jim

This was constructive discussion about the expansion of the concept, not a closure.

"We were full steam ahead at the time. There was definitely going to be a place for the young people and were looking at how to roll out this model in Dundee and South Lanarkshire. There were other Scottish local councils interested in the model. And Jim had the support of the Scottish Government because the model was perceived to be working," says Eddie Hawthorne, the junior college trustee.

An orderly transition was being set in motion with Stewart and Bloomer leading on behalf of the junior college. In June 2018, McColl emailed the council chief saying he understood the transition to move Newlands into the Glasgow Council's education structure was underway.

"I think it would be good if we met from time to time to make sure that the process runs smoothly. Do you have any availability over the next few weeks for a coffee and a catch up?" he offered.

There was genuine excitement that despite all the previous setbacks and acrimony, Glasgow was pressing ahead and the council's chief executive seemed up for the future:

Dear Jim,

I am looking forward to catching up with you tomorrow. I have met with Gerry Lyons our new Head of Service (former Head Teacher of St Andrews and Holyrood) who will oversee the steps to transition the education practice of NJC into the Council, and we have started to develop our thinking about the transition year. I have attached a starter paper on this for your information, which we can discuss further tomorrow.

Regards, Annemarie

The 'starter paper' stated Glasgow City Council was planning the transition of Newlands Junior College's 'provision' into the Education Services' current school estate.

"There is a commitment to learn from the Newlands Junior College experience and the outcomes that it has achieved for young people and ensure that, within our revised provision, this learning is maximised and that the needs of our young people are met in the fullest possible sense within the provision (offer) provided by Education Services."

The context was about increasing focus in Glasgow's schools on a wider, more flexible approach to the curriculum to provide bespoke pathways for individual young people towards higher levels of attainment and achievement and a positive, sustained destinations.

It set out the project's plan for the transition and the enhanced provision for both the young people currently attending Newlands and for those with similar needs in the future. It highlighted something called Aspects of Practice, already in place within Glasgow Schools, which was:

- A commitment to achievement for all;

- A curriculum seen as relevant by students;

- Vocational and personal development aspects of the curriculum.

The report admitted secondary schools were now more focused on delivering an entitlement to achievement for all Glasgow's young people than five years previously.

"More than ever, schools are planning learner journeys to ensure success for all young people. This is evident in the on-going development of the senior phase and the array of alternative curricular models that are being developed for young people in the city."

The focus was increasing the employability of young people with more engagement around the curriculum to enhance and extend vocational pathways with Glasgow's colleges and other business providers. It was spelled out clearly:

"This is absolutely about ensuring that the curriculum is relevant to all young people and, this is particularly the case for young people who are vulnerable and a risk of not achieving. There is very interesting practice in NJC in engaging young people in the design of their curriculum and dialogue around how this is managed would be part of the transition planning process. This is also the case for the Personal Development aspect of the curricular experience offered to young people within NJC."

Newlands Junior College had been leading the charge with its students, showing new levels of motivation and self-confidence, singled out as proof of its success. The report noted the huge uptake in the number of young people achieving external awards out with the Scottish Qualifications Authority, including the Duke of Edinburgh awards, John Muir award, Sports Leadership/Dance Leadership, Personal Development, Leadership and Crest Awards. Furthermore, and at last, the Glasgow starter plan acknowledged the importance of involving the private sector.

> "There is growing partnership with business and schools in Glasgow. The very direct support from the private sector to NJC in terms of providing apprenticeships and employment and we would absolutely want to learn about how to develop that partnership which leads to genuine employment opportunities ... There is growing practice in mentoring through MCR Pathways, Career Ready and others, this would be again important to consider as part of any transitioning programme for young people at Newlands Junior College," stated the council's paper.

Crucial support was needed to help young people arrive at 'positive destinations' with a need to follow-up and support students in those destinations. While Glasgow secondary schools were getting far better at supporting young people into positive destinations there was plenty of room for improvement.

> "Young people transitioning from NJC would receive the same commitment to supporting them in to a positive destination as they currently experience. There is shared learning on how to manage follow up to ensure young people sustain their destinations," said the paper.

The Newlands partnership with City of Glasgow College was central to this. Here was a potential issue to resolve: the provision had been purchased commercially by Newlands and went well beyond the norm of college partnership with Glasgow schools. Who would now pick up this tab? Would this come out of the Glasgow schools budget?

There were also 25 young people directly involved in the transition at Newlands. What would become of them? Many students feared being thrown back into the mainstream schools from which they came. However, there were assurances of proper engagement with each individual young person, their families and carers on planning their learner journey in S2. This transition would be managed in partnership with Newlands and Glasgow Council staff. Learner pathways would be developed to meet the needs of the young people, involving partnership with colleges, schools and employers. Gerry Lyons and colleagues from Glasgow's Education Services would be managing this.

All well and certainly looking good. But there was a deeper issue, which has been placed at the door of Gerry Lyons. It stemmed from the comments made in 2015 by Lyons at the SELMAS conference. Lyons is very well-known in Glasgow and head of one of the biggest schools. He was seconded into Glasgow City Council by Maureen McKenna and he would host discussions with Alex Stewart and Keir Bloomer about Newlands. At the SELMAS conference, McColl flew in directly from abroad missing the morning session, although he had been sent and read a transcript of Chris Kilkenny's talk. After lunch, McColl spoke about Newlands and took some questions, including one from Kilkenny, before leaving. Gerry Lyons was not there in the morning and arrived while McColl was speaking. When Lyons stood up to speak, he had a go at Newlands saying that everything that McColl was claiming already existed in Glasgow's educational circles. It was clear to delegates that Lyons, at this stage, had serious issues with the existence of Newlands. Now three years on, a fault line in the expectations was emerging.

At the start of term in September 2018, there was a college roll of 44, with 21 young people in the Year Two group, while the Year One group had 23, increasing by three to 26, before one student had their scholarship withdrawn. All of their futures were in limbo.

On 1st October 2018, McColl contacted Annemarie O'Donnell on a matter of some urgency.

> *"I am keen that we maintain the momentum as there are a number of issues which will have to be resolved with a degree of urgency. As you know, NJC is currently accommodated within a building owned by SPX. The lease expires in the summer of 2019, so it is extremely important that we identify suitable premises for the college.*

> *"Last week I held a meeting with all the staff at the college to outline the principles of the transition. They are understandably keen to know more details about the changes and how it will affect their future. We have an excellent team at NJC and it is important that we keep them fully informed and feeling secure about their future to ensure a seamless transition for the students. At our last meeting we discussed the essential NJC success factors which are outlined in the attached paper. It is*

important that these factors are firmly embedded in the college going forward. It has had a life changing impact on over 120 young people since we started in 2014.

McColl asked Alex Stewart and Keir Bloomer to arrange a meeting with Gerry Lyons to establish how plans could be made to retain the college's successful components for the next stage of development beyond the pilot and this included finding suitable stand-alone premises. The businessman also suggested the governance structure of junior colleges needed careful consideration, including proper recognition and involvement with the private sector, a continued partnership with Glasgow City Colleges, and more formal involvement of social work services in support for students.

"I believe that it would be a mistake to just slot the Junior Colleges into the existing secondary school structure. I believe that it needs to have its own distinctive staff profile and staff recruitment policy. .. It is extremely important that the Junior Colleges are not seen as special schools. There is a lot to do in the coming months, I appreciate your commitment and support to make this happen," said McColl

A few days later, O'Donnell wrote to McColl in October 2018.

"I had to speak with colleagues to understand their position on discussions to date as your comments did not appear consistent with the discussions we have had on the Council adopting the learning from the NJC into the Education 'offer' once NJC closes in June 2019, aligned to the termination of your lease of the premises.

We have never seen this as a 'transfer' of NJC to the Council along with premises, staff and governance. Any NJC staff wishing to continue in a teaching career would be considered for vacancies within Education Services and we would try to accommodate their preferences wherever possible.

We are currently exploring school and existing college space that might be available to support the success factors from NJC and are having a productive dialogue with Kelvin College at the moment.

I have asked Gerry Lyons to contact Keir to arrange a series of meetings to work through the transition period for our young people to June 2019 and beyond. I'd suggest we have a further discussion once the first draft of this is produced so we can be clear on the communication strategy."

It could be argued that the Council's Chief Executive and the Director of Education's appointees were simply doing their job in protecting the education system in Glasgow. Yet, to the Newlands Junior College team, the 'system' was not doing what was needed for the young people.

In November 2018, Stewart and Bloomer met the transition team in the council offices. They waited for over half an hour while the transition team was in the Executive Director of Education's office. Maureen McKenna was not involved directly with these final negotiations. During this transition meeting, Stewart and Bloomer were informed: *"We're not going to have a separate college, we're going to put them back in the schools where they came from and give them a customised curriculum"*.

This was a bolt from the blue and one which shocked McColl and the junior college trustees.

> "It was just nuts. In an educational and social sense, what could be more important than this? The council and the elected politicians talk about taking people out of poverty but this was one big initiative in Glasgow in lifting people out of poverty. And they didn't do it!"

Twenty-five students would be heading back to places that they already dreaded.

> "Clearly, if we had known we're going to have to send some students back into the mainstream system, then that was not going to be good news for anyone. It was pretty horrific. It was probably one of the saddest days of my life. Knowing what was coming for some of these young people. It was horrible," says Elizabeth Orenes.

Alex Stewart, the deputy chairman of the junior college trustees, wrote to John Swinney [85] saying it was still in his power to *"save what we believe is the most successful and innovative educational development seen in Scotland in recent years"*.

> "The original intention was to test the concept of the junior college over a period of five years. Both the Scottish Government and Glasgow City Council clearly felt that the idea had sufficient merit to justify investing significant sums of public money in it. As that initial five-year trial period draws towards its conclusion, we believe that the validity of the concept has been demonstrated beyond doubt."

---

85 Letter to John Swinney from Alex Stewart, 14 January 2019.

Stewart was not seeking to blame anyone and his tone was gracious, he stated:

> "We recognise the very significant contribution and support from the Scottish Government and Glasgow City Council to the good work that has been done. Surely now is not the time to walk away from this investment? We hope that our leaders in this field, have the courage and vision now to mainstream this project for the benefit of the young people concerned, both now and in the future."

He concluded by saying the young people deserved to be given hope and that closure would be devastating for them. Stewart was supported by letters from the Weir Group and Arnold Clark. Jon Stanton, the chief executive officer of Weir Group, wrote to Swinney saying his company chose to get involved as it addressed a *"clear need to improve the life chances of disadvantaged young people in Glasgow"*. He said the validity of the concept had been demonstrated "beyond doubt", a view corroborated by many educational experts who had visited the junior college. He said that the closure would be a "deeply regrettable result".

Keir Bloomer added his weight saying that the relationships between staff and students have been paramount in the success.

> "This could only be achieved in a small-scale intimate setting where an ethos of trust can be established. I applaud what Glasgow City Council has achieved in terms of raising standards generally but do not believe that provision in mainstream schools can achieve for disengaged young people what is possible in a setting such as Newlands Junior College." [86]

Bloomer urged Swinney not to let a proven concept wither and die, pointing out that while Glasgow was unwilling to sustain a separate junior college, there were several other Scottish local authorities that *"would be eager to set up their own, given a modicum of Scottish Government support"*.

......

Running in parallel with closure was an issue of human resources and options available for Newlands' staff. This can only be described as extremely unsatisfactory, as the Newlands staff, now looking for other employment, were treated badly. For example, Kenny McDonald, the highly-regarded principal science teacher, met with Gerry Lyons in December 2018, and emailed the next day thanking him for the meeting.

---

86 Letter to John Swinney from Keir Bloomer, 14 January 2019.

> McDonald wrote: "*The main points, as I understood them, were: You were fairly certain that, as a Physics teacher, I would have no problem getting a job in Glasgow after the summer. This would keep me for the duration at NJC and, without giving me a full guarantee, you felt that I would be able to walk into a job in Glasgow, you stated that if NJC was to close earlier than expected, e.g. April, then a temporary bridging position would be found for me.*"[87]

Given that STEM (Science, technology, engineering and maths) teaching was increasingly important, and there was a shortage of experienced science teachers, it seemed a post might be in the offing. McDonald appreciated he was on a higher salary scale at Newlands, and Lyons confirmed he could not expect to be kept this level. Lyons said he would find a way of "*keeping you looped in*" about vacancies.

By mid-February 2019, McDonald had been turned down for vacancies as a physics teacher at two Glasgow schools. He was seeking further clarification from Lyons and if he could help with a "*temporary bridging position*". Lyons' curt response was '*leave with me, I'll get back to you.*"

> "Kenny McDonald didn't get a job – and he was placed on a list for relief work, yet didn't get called in. He is an outstanding teacher who did a brilliant job at Newlands, yet the council couldn't find a position for him. I was stunned about this," says Iain White.

He ended up teaching in Motherwell in the North Lanarkshire council area.

One former Newlands team member pointed out that Glasgow Council's Education Services offered assistance to the staff of Craigholme School, an independent all-girls school in Pollokshields which closed in 2020. This was far in access to anything offered to the Newlands teaching staff.

. . . . .

The endgame for the pilot was approaching fast with Alex Stewart leading the college negotiators. At the December trustee meeting, he reported his deep concern that nothing was set in stone. According to Hawthorne, it was becoming clear a whole year of young people at Newlands could be affected with no clear action plan from the council. "*If they are not going to Newlands, where are they going to go?*" pondered the trustees.

From early 2019, the outlook was bleak. McColl called a meeting of the

---

87 Email from Kenny McDonald, December 2018.

trustees and a reluctant decision was made to close the college. The trustees noted in the annual return:

> *"The Glasgow operating college was a five-year project to prove the concept and this was successfully achieved. However, due to funding constraints within the public sector and the non-transfer of the Glasgow operating college to the education authorities, the trustees believed that the required level of private funding would not be able to sustain the ongoing operations. As such it was agreed by the trustees in January 2019 to cease operation of the Glasgow college."* [88]

Iain White remembers being distraught at how quickly this all came to pass. He feels the staff were 'left out' of discussions which led to feelings of resentment and unhappiness as the end approached.

> "In some ways I was removed from the negotiations with Glasgow and wasn't fully aware of what was happening. I admit that caused me some concern because I felt out of the loop. However, my job was to maintain the teaching and the spirit of the college, and in many ways we tried to shield the young people from what was going on behind the scenes. But the decision to close was a shocker for me and for the teaching staff," recalls White.

At the end of January, Newlands Junior College sent a letter to parents and carers saying the college's "demonstration phase" was coming to an end and it had been advised that Glasgow City Council would not give it the resources to put in on a permanent footing and, therefore, there was "no possibility" of continued government funding. The letter continued: *"We appreciate that this announcement will come as a shock and at short notice. NJC was set up as a five-year project to prove that a new and innovative approach to education would work. The project has been amazingly successful with many young people's lives and prospects completely changed. Right up until this week it was hoped that funding could be obtained to continue the project. It has become clear today that there is no possibility of continued government funding."*

The BBC's Scottish education correspondent, Jamie McIvor, quoted Glasgow Council, who pointed the finger of blame at the junior college. A council spokeswoman said: *"The sudden closure of Newlands Junior College must be extremely upsetting for the young people and their families. We are appalled by the way the whole situation has been handled by the Newlands*

---

88 Newlands Junior College, Financial Statement to 30 June 2019. Companies House, 2020.

management team. Letters announcing the closure have been sent out to families out of the blue and without any input from the council."[89]

In the report, a Scottish Government spokesperson said: "*The 2018/19 grant award made it clear that the Scottish Government would make no further contribution to Newlands Junior College's costs, and we expect the college to work with Glasgow City Council to ensure an orderly transition to provision delivered by the council.*"

Without question, the Scottish Government officials in Edinburgh had been extremely supportive of the pilot. However, the official view was that a rigorous and independent evaluation of the college to verify the outcomes was still required.

In October 2019, the author requested a further response and received this email, repeating this point.

> "The Scottish Government was clear in its support and backing for Newlands Junior College. Newlands Junior College delivered learning through an innovative model and there are clear challenges in delivering it on a larger scale and making it financially sustainable. An independent evaluation was a condition of our funding. It is essential that this is completed to ensure we can build on what has been learned at the College, and how this might assist us bridging the attainment gap and delivering positive outcomes for all students in Scotland." [90]

Keir Bloomer was interviewed in the *Sunday Times* [91] questioning whether Scotland's schooling system was capable of "any serious innovation".

> "At the time when they were admitted, almost all seemed destined to fail. However, everyone who completed the two-year course is employed in an apprenticeship or on a college course. The benefits are huge, both for the young people themselves and for society. In the end, being a proven success story was not enough. An education system that is disturbingly short of successes hasn't been able to keep this one going. It is tempting, but futile, to allocate blame. Much more important is to learn lessons and build into the system a capacity for bold and successful innovation in the future," he told the reporter Shingi Maraike.

89 Row over closure of Glasgow entrepreneur's vocational school, BBC, 1 February 2019.
www.bbc.co.uk/news/uk-scotland-glasgow-west-47094231
90 Email from Scottish Government, 5 October 2019.
91 The Sunday Times, 3 February 2019.

In reply, a Scottish Government spokesman repeated:

> "There has been no independent evaluation of the outcomes achieved by Newlands Junior College. The completion of such an evaluation is a condition of the funding provided by the Scottish Government. There are many excellent examples of innovation throughout Scotland's education system."

When the trustees gathered in March 2019, there was one emergency item on the top of the agenda. What will happen to the young people? And what about their families?

> "What about the kids? How can we ensure the best transition for them? We had the second year, who all had a positive destination that they were working towards, but the first years were too early for the positive destinations, so it was how many are going to mainstream school," recalls Hawthorne.

With some irony, Glasgow's Education Services were being lauded in March by Education Scotland's inspectors for "an excellent report card" and improving learning and raising attainment across the city. It stated that 92.3% of the city's pupils, the highest on record, had gone on to "positive destinations". The glowing report also stated: "The Executive Director of Education's leadership is founded on her passion, commitment and relentless drive to reduce the impact of poverty on the outcome of all children and young people."

Councillor Chris Cunningham, the convener for education, skills & early years, was clearly delighted: "The improvements in the learning and teaching in our schools over the last 10 years are nothing short of remarkable." High and effusive praise indeed and, undoubtedly, deserved in the wider context. Yet such endorsement felt very hollow in the environs of Newlands, where the critical question was: how long could they keep the college open?

In effect, the junior college managed to keep several students on until the end of May 2019, to help them through their exams, rather than returning them to mainstream schools. This depended on keeping the college solvent. Hawthorne explains that business supporters and individuals took up the slack.

> "Towards the end a lot of the business and individual contributors paid in more than they were expecting to, just to ease the transition, but that was after we found out that the council had different plans. I was

never involved in any of the discussion with Glasgow council, so as a trustee I was hearing it from Jim and Alex, who I trusted to relay the right information. I firmly believe they were being told that this pilot was something that the council was going to take on because it was a success," he says.

.....

Friday, 26th April 2019 was a red letter day for Newlands Junior College. There was immense pride tinged with sadness. Elizabeth Orenes' first experience of a Newlands' Graduation ceremony had been at the City of Glasgow College a year earlier which she felt it was a bit too structured and stuffy. Although she admitted it was a highly significant public occasion for the junior college in the brand new mega-college. However, the fourth and final graduation was in Inverlair Avenue, Cathcart, back where it all started, and this, she felt, was a more appropriate and intimate event. There were 11 young people who graduated on this day.

The ceremony began at 10am with a welcome from Philip Graham, an address from Jim McColl and then some wise words from Iain White. There was the presentation of both subject and vocational awards, and Carol Henry, head of human resources at Arnold Clark, and a director of the Glasgow Chamber of Commerce, handed out the certificates of achievement.

> "There was a conscious decision not to make it sad or angry because the college was closing. This was something we had to be very careful about. We did not want to make a fuss or big noise about the closure, because that would not really help anyone," says Orenes.

Philip Graham was very clear that the day had to be about the pupils' achievements and should not be used as a public relations platform to criticise the powers-that-be.

> "The students deserved their day. It was a very important day and a very proud day for them, and for their parents," says Orenes.

After the ceremony, the students, parents and carers enjoyed a buffet lunch, while everyone was laughing and smiling as 'selfies' with friends and family and teachers were snapped on their mobile phones. It was a poignant ending as the junior college emptied out with farewell hugs and goodbyes. By 2pm, the college was empty and silent.

Later that afternoon, a video was posted on the college's Facebook page:

"This quiet, five-minute walkthrough of the empty NJC building in no way reflects the triumphs or the disappointments, nor the fun, laughter and happy, noisy chaos that the NJC family has experienced within its walls. We do hope however that it will give those that worked with us or visited us over the last five years, a chance to remember just what we all achieved here."

All that can be heard on the video is the footsteps and the automatic doors opening to leave. It's like a modern-day Marie Celeste. The post referred to Lee Iacocca, the Ford executive and latterly Chrysler Cars CEO, who was quoted as saying *"The thing that lies at the foundation of positive change, the way I see it, is service to a fellow human being"* and then it continued.

"As Philip, our Depute Principal, reiterated at today's graduation ceremony, NJC was always only ever about one thing; service to and for the benefit of the students. This is not the end of the NJC story, it is merely the beginning of a new chapter. Exciting times lie ahead for all of our graduates and we can't wait to hear how they all get on."

Finally, the post quoted the Greek writer and activist, Dinos Christianopoulos, who came up with the memorable saying used by Mexicans protesting at the disappearance of students in 2013: *'They tried to bury us. They did not know we were seeds'*. Gillian Hunt in a Facebook 'like' responded:

"It has been my absolute privilege to be part of Newlands Junior College. I have learned so much from the amazing young people there. Everyone involved has kept them at the heart of all they do. What a place! Congratulations on the graduation celebration, it was a wonderful event. All the very best to each of you. Gillian."

CHAPTER TWENTY-THREE

Shock and Dismay: The Pilot Spurned

There was dismay and disappointment at the decision. In May 2019, all of the college's remaining staff, the five academic and two people in administrative, were made redundant.

> "The pilot was always going to end after five years. What is disappointing is that it did not continue in the way Glasgow City Council said they would continue with it, even in the final year," says Stewart.

With the college seeking new applications for the 2018/2019 session, the council's dithering on its future was a deterrent for head teachers considering nominating pupils for the final year. It was also a barrier to new investment from business people who, despite learning of the tangible success, were not going to support a college with an uncertain future.

> "It was only later on in the life of the junior college that we had a track record and successful examples we could show to funders as a demonstration. This was all about students coming from disadvantaged backgrounds and whose lives had been turned around. It was then that the conversations with potential funders, who had originally declined to become involved, became more real," says Scott Black.

All of this was too late for Newlands. As a trustee, Black was given the remit to attract more private sector funders.

> "It was evident from early on that Glasgow City Council were not keen on a standalone college. Whether it ran the risk of showing them up, or because philosophically they were against any form of private education, they weren't for it and their support was pretty limited. It was always a chore to even get the little money we received out of them," says Black.

Alex Stewart's view is that Scotland's secondary education system is flawed because there is little room for innovation, new thinking and fresh streams of investment. This was a concern before the COVID-19 pandemic disrupted education in Scotland, but as the new term approached in the late summer of 2020, education authorities were being forced to come to terms with a 'new normal' of teaching and learning. Education authorities, who were rightly trying to prevent the spread of a deadly virus, were forced to retreat from a position of 'blended learning' where more pupils would use technology and video calls in their homes rather than attending their schools for the full week.

This sparked a widespread backlash from parents across Scotland who were already adapting to new modes of home working, and the prospect of furloughing and unemployment, while more vulnerable pupils were losing out on formal learning.

Speaking before the COVID-19 lockdown, Alex Stewart was prescient in arguing that radical change was required in the funding of Scotland's education.

> "You cannot allocate a budget for the country based on last year and allow for any real change. We could not unlock money from other budgets such as Community and Place, Criminal Justice and Social Work, even though we were going to save them a fortune," he says.

Stewart, a seasoned chartered accountant, accepts the point made by Maureen McKenna when she stated there were no savings to her education department budget, and that if other council departments wanted to support a junior college, then it should come from their council budgets.

> "She says it's going to cost her budget money. She is right in that respect. All the savings are almost in every other budgets, such as Criminal Justice, Social Work and the NHS and on the Benefits costs. The savings are enormous for these young people. I get her point but the savings would be to other budgets and not the education one," he says.

In retrospect, Keir Bloomer believes that supporting a future network of junior colleges across Scotland will require a different form of funding.

> "I always felt criticism of the public sector was a little unfair because the Scottish Government and Glasgow City Council invariably paid what they were asked to pay," he says.

A much bolder approach was necessary with different calculations about an individuals' entitlement to education, so that the more disadvantaged were given a fairer share of the total educational budget, and that other budgets, including Social Work, Criminal Justice and National Health Service were also utilised.

"It seemed to be a really difficult and unsolvable problem of how do we get a blend of funding from various sources, not simply the educational budget. It seemed that there was resistance in certain local authorities who had an underlying problem with the concept of private schooling," says Black.

A key lesson learned by Scott Black is that business people need to be very careful about how they position proposals when dealing with matters of education and social care.

"You need to try and understand from the get-go what are all the factors running through the heads of the educational authority and council chiefs. From our perspective, it seemed to be a no-brainer, because if you can do something that helps some of those children to achieve their potential to go onto a positive destination, then it was worth trying because the impact of them not achieving had such a negative impact on society. It seemed such an obvious equation to me."

Perhaps it was preaching to the converted, but this was debated time and again around the table at trustee meetings.

"Why can't the elected councillors and the executives within Glasgow City Council understand that if one of these young people falls out of the school system into drugs, abuse or crime, then they end up costing society a fortune? Why was this not so obvious?" ponders Black.

The quibbling with the local government went on and finally McColl underwrote the Santander Bank overdraft of £500,000, paying it off out of Clyde Blowers Capital funds. Yet Newlands Junior College supporters remained dismayed about how and why it all folded.

So what was the official response? It was clear there was another side to the argument. On 26th November 2019, in the process of writing this book, a series of questions were posed to Glasgow City Council, to answer some of the claims made by those interviewed for this book. A request for on-the-record comments and an interview with the Executive Director of Education was also made.

"I would also very much appreciate the cooperation of Glasgow City Council and its Department of Education in the clarification and response to a number of points," said the author.

In early February 2020, after a further email, a polite response came from the communications officer saying: *"I'm afraid that we are also going to decline your invitation to take part in the interview for the book after a discussion with the chief executive's office."* [92]

These 14 points were unanswered by the council.

- The College was intended to be a five-year pilot project in 'partnership' with Glasgow City Council, but many of those associated with the College claim that Glasgow's Director of Education was completely against its operation and development from the very start. Is this a fair characterisation to make?

- Can Glasgow Council confirm that the Newlands Junior College was indeed a 'partnership' project which had the full support of Glasgow's Education Department?

- There were fundamental differences of views between the business founder of the college and the Director of Education and disagreement over whether a college of this type was required in Glasgow. Is this a fair comment to make?

- There is a claim that the Director of Education made it clear to Head Teachers in Glasgow that she would not be happy with Head Teachers recommending pupils to transfer to Newlands Junior College. Is this true? If so, what were her reasons?

- If this was indeed a 'partnership' project, why were so many Head Teachers in Glasgow vehemently opposed to agreeing to send suitable students to Newlands?

- I have been told that from the outset, the College was set higher hurdles on specifying course material and teaching facilities than any other educational establishments in Glasgow. Is this a fair point? If so, why were these higher standards required?

- While the movement of teaching staff from Govan High School to the Newlands Junior College had a detrimental impact on Govan High, the Director of Education made personal statements towards certain

---

92 Email from City of Glasgow Council, February 2020.

teaching staff who made the move. What concerns did the Director have about this and why were such statements necessary?

• It has been suggested that personal animosity from senior figures in the education department existed towards certain members of the teaching staff at Newlands and this tainted ongoing relationships and the progress of the college. Is this a fair assessment?

• I understand the Director of Education never attended any of the college graduation ceremonies despite repeated invitations? Is it fair to say the college was being snubbed?

• In the education department's view, what were the main reasons for withdrawing support for a separate stand-alone junior college of this nature?

• Why did Glasgow Department of Education choose to recommend its closure?

• Could you confirm the exact financial contributions made to the College over its five-year existence?

• Did the Council undertake an evaluation of the College and the future cost of taking it on? Could I be sent a copy of this evaluation?

• How did the Education Department officials feel about returning students to the schools where they originally came from – and what assessment was done on this to protect the young people concerned?

The reader can draw their own conclusions about why Glasgow's officials did not see it important to respond. The author considered filing a Freedom of Information request to seek some further clarification, but felt that the polite stonewalling was enough testimony to show the readers the unwillingness of the local authority to engage in answering legitimate and reasonable questions.

CHAPTER TWENTY-FOUR:
You Can't Defeat the Empire – Or Can You?

The tiny junior college was squeezed out of existence. The educational conditions applied to Newlands Junior College were never the same as those for Glasgow's mainstream educational establishments. The junior college had been forced to give a guarantee about the positive destination of the young people after they left the college.

Yet the definition of a 'positive destination' from Newlands was a much tougher achievement, than the 'positive destinations' for Glasgow's secondary schools, where a 'positive destination' could be equated to nothing more than a six-week training course.

"We were not allowed that as a 'positive destination', we had to make it a real apprenticeship, a real full-time job, or a real place in the full-time college system," says Alex Stewart. "And this was thrown against us in the end. We had to guarantee a positive outcome as long as the child does the two years and stays with us. We did lose a few, but this was a tiny minority. But some of the kids have been real challenges and yet stuck with us."

Scottish Government statistics measure positive destinations only once, shortly after the young people leave school — a point of data collection which needs to be seriously addressed. A year or two years later, many less committed young people will have dropped out.

Yet Graham Robertson's mentoring and follow-up work at Newlands ensured that former students showed greater resilience or 'stickability'. This Newlands Junior College 'after sales service' was not limited to employability and further education. Where students request it, mentoring continues to the present day, even after the closure. There have even been instances where former staff have intervened directly and swiftly to save students from the threat of homelessness. No doubt many mainstream schools can give instances where they have been able to help former pupils but Newlands Junior College's efforts were unique in their level of organisation and inclusiveness.

Despite all this good work, Alex Stewart, a man of considerable international business experience, who had fought and secured major deals across the globe, admitted: *"It's impossible to defeat the Empire. You can't defeat it."* Yet the statistics from the college were impressive. But, more importantly, it was about young lives and Newlands Junior College reported regularly to the Scottish Government about its achievements. *"The fact is that the college achieved very high levels of success,"* states Bloomer.

Certainly, as described in this book, Newlands was not catering for the most disruptive pupils or the so-called "bampots", but this was no pushover. The criteria for admission remained: that the young person had to be disengaged or appear to be disengaged from traditional schooling; they had to have some evidence of potential, perhaps from an earlier stage in their education; and there had to be reasonable grounds for thinking they would benefit from the junior college experience.

> "There are people who are disengaged and have never shown any potential. They were violent or actively anti-social. Newlands never dealt with this extreme anti-social group. This is not a criticism of the college, because it was serving a perfectly specific group with whom it achieved a very good level of success," says Bloomer.

Bloomer accepts that it could be seen as *"eroding the cycle of educational disadvantage from the easier end "*, while other critics simply dismissed the college as *"cherry-picking winners"*.

Eddie Hawthorne doesn't see it like this. His view is that mainstream education is fine and he makes no criticism of it — or what the local councils are providing for 95% of the pupils. But the remaining 5% don't quite make it.

> "Jim's point was if we can help these young people get back on track, then not only are we helping them and their families, we are giving them a better life, we're proving that the pilot works and we are also saving society money. Because if these young people don't have the future it costs society in the long-run looking after them," says Hawthorne.

It is worth repeating the findings of Gillian Hunt's research here:

> "Over its five years of operation, 134 students attended Newlands Junior College. At the time of its closure, 26 students were in the middle of their courses and were returned to local authority schools to complete their statutory education as they were not yet 16. During the course of its five years, 19 students returned to local authority schools for a variety of reasons. Of the 89 students who completed their education at

Newlands, 92.1% went on to a positive destination; further education, an apprenticeship or a job. This is an outstanding achievement."

As explained previously, the 19 students who returned to local authority schools did so for a variety of reasons. One pertinent point is that Newlands Junior College had a privilege enjoyed by all independent schools in that it was able to 'choose' not to educate a young person. In contrast, Glasgow City Council has a statutory 'obligation' which it cannot shake and must try to find a place to educate people, no matter their misdemeanours. It is unknown to Newlands whether these students entered positive destinations or not. However, those in the middle of their Newlands' courses, who returned to the mainstream because they were not yet 16, had been given a glimpse of hope and opportunity.

"It should be noted that a return to local authority for a good number of students was a positive destination. Some of those returning did so after a renewed appetite for learning, improved confidence and an ability to attend school, and returned to continue studies in S5 and S6," says Hunt.

In conclusion, the percentage of young people reaching 'positive destinations', who had any contact with Newlands Junior College, was a minimum of 75.9%, three times the 25% rate of success predicted by their original mainstream schools. Yet, to rightly assess the junior college's success rate, we need to measure those who completed their two-year courses and fully attended to gain the maximum benefit. This figure is 92.1%.

The challenge for the trustees was to make sure that everyone had a positive outcome, whether that be an apprenticeship, further education through college course, or a normal full-time job. *"For someone who wasn't destined to get a job, this is a huge thing,"* says Eddie Hawthorne. While Scott Black originally considered half of the students making it into a positive destination would be a strong achievement, he felt that 92.1% was, indeed, remarkable and worthy of celebration.

"There was one example of a boy in the final year. His attendance at a previous secondary school was zero. Yet his attendance at Newlands was 100%. It's always easy to find one and say there is a fantastic statistic, let's talk about this," says Black.

While 100% attendance was exemplary, the majority of students were turning up regularly and on time. Something special was happening at Newlands that made these people turn up — and it wasn't simply being picked up by the minibus every morning, although this was an important factor.

"There was something else that made them attend every day. If they were that disruptive they wouldn't get on the bus. So, first of all, let's talk about Newlands as a *positive d*estination. This wasn't because it was a free-for-all carnival atmosphere. They were working hard and the academic results of the college demonstrated this," he adds.

He argues that even an attendance rate of 60 to 70% rate over three years is an incredible improvement.

"These people would be on Welfare, they might be on drugs or in the criminal justice system, or in ill-health. What we did was we fed them healthy meals every day. You could see the change in the energy levels. So diet was a big part of it. This helps with attention span and an ability to concentrate for longer. But the biggest thing was making them feel good about themselves," he says.

The students started to push themselves back into the academic system and their exam success was a part, but not all, of the proof. Does he still believe the Newlands Junior College model has a future?

"Yes, absolutely. There is an obvious place for this kind of establishment. It's a no-brainer. I can understand why the Scottish Government with many conflicting priorities might consider it too hard to implement and roll-out. But the creation of Newlands Junior College was one of the most enlightened things I have come across in Scotland in recent years. If, as an education system, you are seeking to latch onto some bright spots or flagship projects, this could be one," adds Black.

In Black's views, it should not be beyond concerned people in Scotland to understand the obvious benefits of the Newlands idea and work out how to make it affordable and workable across the country.

And what about Alex Stewart? McColl's close colleague who was reluctantly drawn into the project against his better judgement?

"I'm so glad we did it because in some ways it is one of the most rewarding things I have ever been involved with. I ended up in the college many times during the week and ended up teaching two classes. To this day, I stay in touch with several of the students and have continued mentoring them. I've got to know them really well. I became the opposite of the atheist, I became the believer!" he says.

In many hearts, the Newlands Junior College concept is only dormant. The lessons learned are about how to engage with local authorities, their directors of education and head teachers to properly articulate why this must be considered as part of Scotland's educational future.

Keir Bloomer, writing in his letter to John Swinney in January 2019, [93] was sure the opportunity should not be lost.

> "Looking more widely, the issue here is about innovation in Scottish education. No objective observer now disputes the need for significant change. Yet here is an innovation lauded across the political spectrum that seems likely to die because of a lack of will to see it continued."

He feared that the closure of Newlands would be seen as proof that Scottish education is *"incapable of sustaining innovation even where results are highly positive and political opinion, across party divisions, agrees that the benefits to underprivileged young people have been clearly established."*

Even after the closure of the Cathcart establishment, senior Clyde Blowers figures are mentoring the cohort to ensure that they remain on track. Arnold Clark's Hawthorne was asked: *"Would he do it again?"*

"Yes, for the kids. But for the council and the politics, no," he says.

What could be done differently?

> "Proper commitment upfront from the Scottish Government and the local authority, that's about a defined commitment to either providing the facility or they take it over," he says. "People need to believe in it, and I'm not sure Glasgow's education department ever did."

> "We are continuing to support the young people who attended Newlands Junior College and we are also continuing to support any new local councils that want to set up a junior college using our template. It is a matter of how we franchise this. It needs to be with local authorities," he says.

McColl has not given up either. He hopes that politicians with fresh eyes and hearing and seeing the benefits will see the merits and take it over as a Scottish Government project as a subset of the further education and college sector. But he has expressed a fear that the Newlands Junior College model had become a 'toxic brand' in some council educational circles.

> "Maybe in the way they allocate the budgets to councils can be based on individual amounts of £7,600 per person. This is all that they should

93 Letter to John Swinney from Keir Bloomer, 14 January 2019.

get. We were taking people away from mainstream secondary schools yet the schools were still getting around £7,600 per head. They could be smarter in the way they do that, so that the money is attached to the pupil throughout their school journey."

Alex Stewart agrees and believes it remains a fundamental and unresolved matter of inclusion for disadvantaged young people and fairness.

"At the end, we were told we are elitist and selective and that everyone should be treated the same, but those who were coming to Newlands were not getting their fair share until they came to the college. They were not getting the money spent on them, yet they were coming from the poorest parts of the city."

He also says having access to the Pupil Equity Fund, which was attached to each learner, could have been deployed to help support the junior college.

"To my despair, we would sit in meetings at Victoria Quay in Edinburgh and in Glasgow and talk about money and budgets, we would talk about the system and private sector versus public sector, but it drove me up the wall because one of the last things we ever talked about was the individual child who makes up this body. This drives you to despair eventually," he says.

How does McColl view the five years?

"In my view, it was a complete success. We proved the model that we set out to prove. It was only ever going to be for five years and then it was going to be taken into the public education system. It was successful, but it didn't get adopted. It was funded by ourselves and the business people we approached. The amount that the Scottish Government, which was purely for set-up costs, and the local authorities gave us was never going to be enough."

There is no doubt this kind of provision will cost more than a mainstream school. The Stewart/McColl argument is young people who stay on for S5 and S6 get a better educational deal. If all pupils across Scotland were entitled to six years, then those at the end of S2 should have four years of credits left.

"This could mean that this cohort of young people have two years in a mainstream secondary and then two years at a junior college, resulting in a guaranteed positive destination. Why shouldn't those young people who are being let down by the mainstream system have the opportunity to attend a junior college? It's a logical question which required a coherent answer from the education authorities if they are sincere in wanting to create more equality in society," says McColl.

The figures were set out in a report commissioned after Newlands' pilot years were completed.

"At Newlands Junior College the cost was around £15,000, though this would decrease significantly if the college were able to make use of local authority support services. A student attending S1 to S4 in mainstream schooling costs around £27,000 and attending S1 to S6 around £41,000. If students then attend university the total cost is around £77,000. Although the cost to educate a young person at a junior college is higher, the difference is that the investment of two years at a junior college leads to much higher levels of success, with the cost of their four years of education (two years in mainstream and two years in a junior college) being around £44,000," explained Gillian Hunt. [94]

From Black's point of view, such arguments made by McColl and Stewart were the logical ones. The deep frustration was about the lack of joined-up thinking across various budgets, rather than funding stuck in silos. He witnessed this personally when he went to speak with the directors of education at City of Edinburgh Council and Stirling Council.

"Very quickly, I found myself in an identical conversation. I found the people we spoke to understood where we were coming from and, for the most part, were sympathetic to what we were saying," he says.

But there was a feeling that Newlands' card had been marked in educational circles and it was becoming a toxic brand in other councils. It always seemed to return to the money and the average figure of £7,600 a year to have a Scottish secondary pupil in school [the primary school figure is only around £5,000], as opposed to the £15,000 a year in Newlands Junior College.

"The savings are short-term because these are people who are falling out the system now, not in three weeks' time. This is happening now. So the cost burden is now, not in three years' time. Children are costing the state three or four time the burden now."

Meanwhile, youth unemployment remains a deep-seated international issue. The issue of COVID-19 and the unprecedented changes to the major European

94 Newlands Junior College, 2014-2019, Report 2020.

economies will make it far harder for those at the bottom end of the job market with no qualifications or work experience. According to the Eurostat database, around 15 million young people aged 20-34 were neither in employment, nor education and training within the EU-28 nations in 2018. In Italy and Greece, with the highest youth unemployment rate, more than a quarter of young people were out of the labour force. Throughout 2020, as Scotland hunkered down to deal with the global pandemic, there were daunting discussions about what kind of world would emerge. What is of increasing concern is that the vocational opportunities for many young people might disappear in the longer term as businesses and not-for-profit organisations go under.

Alex Stewart pessimistically said it was impossible to defeat the empire. But when Scotland properly emerges from the shocking virus that has devastated lives and impacted severely on the society, radical innovation in education will be desperately required. There will be a realisation that it will be those vulnerable people previously served by Newlands Junior College who are in greatest danger of falling behind.

According to *The Observer* newspaper report in October 2020 [95], almost one million vulnerable 16 to 24-year-olds who are not in full-time education or employment *"will face significant barriers to work"* when the furlough scheme introduced to protect jobs during the pandemic ended at the end of that month. Research by Professor Paul Gregg, at Bath University, pointed out that a scarcity of new positions and the arrival of school and college leavers in the job market presented young people with bleak prospects for their future. Former Prime Minister Gordon Brown, Premier between 2007 and 2010, wrote in the same newspaper that the COVID-19 generation could be as *"desolate and as neglected as the YTS (Youth Training Scheme) generation in the 1980s."*

So perhaps, as the education system buckles under this strain and more young people face the prospects of leaving secondary education without a positive employment destination, the time has come to invest in new thinking and build a network of junior colleges around our nation.

Perhaps Scotland's teaching professionals will step up again to ensure, once and for all, the rightful inclusion of all young people. I'm sure then they might wholeheartedly embrace the idea, the innovation and the life-changing endeavour that was Newlands Junior College.

---

95 The Observer, 18 October 2020.

ACKNOWLEDGEMENTS

The author would like to acknowledge the support of various people who have co-operated with the writing of this book. Iain White for giving up his time to explain more about teaching in Scotland and his unique journey to become the Principal at Newlands Junior College. Thank you also to Philip Graham, who can only be described as an exemplary educator who was admired by Newlands staff and students in equal measure. If White & Graham were a Scotch whisky, they would be bottled as a 'premium blend'. Thanks too to Elizabeth Orenes for organising interviews with students, former students and with the local community. Thanks to Keir Bloomer, Gillian Hunt, the Rev Wilma Pearson, Donald Macleod, Angela Meikle and Karen Hamilton. Thanks to the trustees, Scott Black, Eddie Hawthorne and a special thanks to Alex Stewart. Most of all, thanks to all the students who have spoken on and off the record, your unstinting praise for Newlands is the best testimony.

…..

Writer's endnote: I am a Scottish-based writer and journalist and was commissioned by Jim McColl to collect the interviews and put this into a book about Newlands Junior College. My mother was a Scottish primary school teacher who spent 25 years in the classroom at Stenhouse and then Carrick Knowe in Edinburgh. She dealt with several Primary year groups. Her brother, my uncle, was Deputy head teacher at Oban High School, then one of the largest secondaries in the Highlands. So I fully understand that school teaching is an arduous and tiring occupation. Studies show that teachers working in areas of deprivation, poverty, and high-crime have higher levels of stress and are more liable to burn-out. The lack of support given to teachers working in severely under-resourced communities has been shown to lead to high rates of teacher turnover. It takes committed and remarkable people to thrive and create daily order and calm amid constant disruption and disorder. I have the utmost respect for teachers. Any criticism in this book refers to the strategies and policies of educational authorities and their inflexibility in their ability to deal with change. Finally, I'd like to thank Jim McColl for this commission and I'm grateful for his input and comments.

Kenny Kemp, April 2021

About the author: Kenny Kemp is an award-winning Scottish writer and journalist. He was a former staff journalist on the London *Evening Standard*, *The Scotsman*, and was the founding Business Editor of the *Sunday Herald*. He has written several works of non-fiction, including ghost-written biographies. He was co-author of *Go: An Airline Adventure*, which won WH Smith Business Book of the Year in 2004. He has been Scottish Business Writer of the Year three times, most recently in 2010. An Economic History and Politics graduate of University of Strathclyde, he is an Associate of the University of Edinburgh Business School. He lives in Edinburgh.

Index